The Dark Temple

A Basic Fantasy Role-Playing Game Adventure Series
For Player Characters of Various Levels

Copyright © 2019-2022 Chris Gonnerman and Contributors. All Rights Reserved.
Distributed under the terms of the Open Game License version 1.0a

1st Edition (Release 14)

www.basicfantasy.org

Credits

Contributors: Kyle Hettinger, Russ Robinson, Sean Wellington, Alan Vetter, Clinton L. Robison, and James Lemon

Proofing: Alan Vetter, James Lemon, JD Neal, Gavin Rourke, and Chris Gonnerman

Cover Art: John Fredericks

Art: Stephen Trenkamp, Alexander Cook, Andrés Cuesta, Gabe Fua, MWByouk, Martín Serena, Colin Richards, Leon Atkinson, Andy "ATOM" Taylor, Mike Hill, and Brian DeClerq

Maps: Borgar Olsen and Pytheas

Introduction

The Dark Temple is the second adventure multimodule in the **Basic Fantasy Contest Series.** Like the original contest adventure series, **Castle by the Sea**, this work consists of a set of adventures all written to use the same set of dungeon maps. The adventures are compact, most being playable in full in one to three sessions.

All contestants were asked to create a dungeon key using the provided maps and this writing prompt: **A temple, ancient and crumbling, haunted by some eldritch horror**. Six adventures were submitted for the contest, to be decided on by a vote open to all forum members. In the end two adventures, The Horror Within and The Children of Zewlac, tied for first place. Thus it fell to me to cast the tie-breaking vote, and after spending a day considering these two front-runners I selected the winner: **The Children of Zewlac** by Kyle Hettinger.

All six adventures are presented below, led by the winner and followed by the others in descending order by votes received (and by order of submission for those that tied). Only one could win, but I believe that all six are fun, interesting, and challenging adventures, and I look forward to play-testing every one of them. I hope that you too will find them worthy!

Chris Gonnerman
October 2019

Player's Introduction

Below is the original player's introduction as written for the contest. Contestants were permitted to change this description, so before reading it to your players, please review the specific adventure you plan to run.

The temple stands on a rocky prominence overlooking the sea, a week's ride north of Slateholm. Once long ago a thriving town was nearby, and the townsfolk came to the temple to give tribute to the sea god; but the town was overrun in the first Goblin War, and the temple sacked and turned into a hobgoblin fortress. After the hobgoblins were vanquished, the temple lay empty most of a hundred years before, according to rumors, another priesthood came to the temple and began repairing it. But these priests were secretive and more than a little ominous, and those trappers and hunters who frequented the region gave the temple a wide berth. Over the next few years, the priests were seen less and less, until finally all assumed they had died out.

Lately, though, strange tales have begun to circulate about *things* half-seen within the temple, or lurking in the woods nearby…

*If you might be a player in this adventure, **stop reading now!***
Beyond this point lies information meant only for the Game Master's eyes!

Game Master's Introduction

This contest, like the Castle by the Sea contest, presented the contestants with a set of maps for a dungeon environment. This dungeon has three levels: The upper level, i.e. the eponymous dark (and crumbling) temple; the middle level, consisting of several rooms that actually span several "levels" vertically; and the lower level, where the really creepy and/or nasty stuff probably lives. Some additional descriptive text (presented below) was given, but participants were allowed to make any changes they desired so long as no actual changes were made to any maps.

The roof of the sanctuary (area 14) was wooden, covered with wooden shakes (shingles); it has rotted away almost completely, leaving the entire space open to the sky. The roof over the foyer (2) is the same material, but more of it still stands, though with a few large holes in it. The frame supporting the roof over the wings is stone, being the buttresses that support the sanctuary walls, and for that reason the roofing there is mostly intact but more than a little leaky.

Note that the adventures presented in this book include monsters from the **Basic Fantasy Field Guide Volumes 1** through **3**, as well as items from the **Basic Fantasy Equipment Emporium**. All of these books are available for free on our website, **www.basicfantasy.org**, along with many other resources to enhance and expand your Basic Fantasy RPG campaign.

The Adventures

The Children of Zewlac

by Kyle Hettinger

———————— *Winner of the Dark Temple contest!* ————————

Introduction

The temple stands on a rocky prominence overlooking the sea, a week's ride north of Slateholm. Once long ago a thriving town was nearby, and the townsfolk came to the temple to give tribute to the Old Sea God; but the town was overrun in the first Goblin War, and the temple sacked and turned into a hobgoblin fortress. After the hobgoblins were vanquished nearly a century ago, the temple lay empty. By that time, the Old Sea God and his assemblage of queer saints had been all but forgotten by the local population, replaced by a more modern, respectable pantheon. Today the temple is simply known as "The Dark Temple".

Recently, though, a strange cult has taken up residence in the temple. This new cult is led by a man named "Zewlac". Despite the cultists' unsettling appearance and beliefs, the cult poses no obvious threat to the community other than winning the occasional convert from the dominant faiths.

Apart from these recent Zewlac cultists, the temple hasn't been visited in years. In the minds of most locals it is the subject of superstition and ghost stories told to frighten children, **a temple, ancient and crumbling, haunted by some eldritch horror...**

What's Going On Here?

Up until recently, the Dark Temple had lain abandoned. Recent events began with Gregory, a charcoal-burner living a few miles from the old temple. One night Gregory received a revelation. Known only to him, this "revelation" consisted of an encounter with a werecockroach who infected him with lycanthropy. He started avoiding daylight, developed some new ideas, and renamed himself "Zewlac". He became completely nocturnal, spending his evenings in the village square preaching a gospel of spiritual liberation and poor hygiene.

A local woman, Elinor, became an early disciple. When she succumbed to Zewlac's charms and absconded with him, she donated her jewelry and other savings to his cult. With the proceeds, Zewlac approached the local rulers to purchase the dilapidated, unfrequented seaside temple. He promptly moved in with a small group of followers. Lately he's been winning more converts from the village of St. Dagon's Cove and the surrounding countryside. These "Zewlac-cultists" are mostly drawn from lowly fishermen and peasants, people more than happy to leave their lives of drudgery for the carefree squalor of the Zewlac cult.

The Zewlac-cultists occupy the temple's upper and middle levels. Elinor has fallen out of favor with the group and fled to the temple's lower level. That level, sealed off from the rest of the complex with a magical ward, contains more ancient, vengeful beings associated with the Old Sea God. Elinor herself fell prey to one of these beings, and is now possessed by an evil spirit. Her estranged husband wants her home safe and sound, but accomplishing that might prove difficult.

Notes for the GM

This adventure offers opportunities for role-playing, hack-and-slash, or both, depending on the party's temperament. An adventure hook is provided in the following description of the village of St. Dagon's Cove, but the GM may motivate players in other ways. Bloodthirsty parties might have a jolly time wading into battle in a temple full of raging cultists. Alternatively, orthodox clerics and paladin-types may just seek to wipe out an evil, heretical sect.

St. Dagon's Cove

As an adventure hook, the GM may have the players begin at St. Dagon's Cove, a coastal village 3 miles from the Dark Temple.

St. Dagon's Cove has a population of just over 400, most of whom earn their livelihood through the fishing trade. Its streets and docks are surprisingly well-maintained and clean, reflecting a population that is both serious and hardworking. At night, many enjoy unwinding at the village's only tavern: the Spoiled Mermaid. Any strangers in town are sure to be pointed in that direction.

The GM may substitute a different settlement, or skip a beginning town entirely, but the following sections provide possible resources for adventurers as well as a hook to engage the players.

THE SPOILED MERMAID

Set amid a street of row houses down by the docks, this structure is perhaps the largest in the village. The outside placard depicts the stereotypical mermaid: long red hair, breasts tastefully covered in clam shells, and green fish scales and fin in the place of the maid's lower half. But unlike the stereotypical mermaid, this mermaid's face is twisted in an expression of scorn, her tongue sticking out.

The front door to the inn opens directly into the bar, which is smoke-filled and occupied at all times of day, only growing crowded after the fishing boats return in the late afternoon.

At *The Spoiled Mermaid* inn and public house a guest can rent a cramped single room for 5 sp a night or a cot in the smoky common room for 8 cp. Tavern fare is cod or clam chowder for 1 sp and a pint of beer for 4 cp. It is owned by Mother Mame, a stout but energetic woman with one eye and a heart of gold.

The bar is typically stuffed with drunken fishermen, and can be rough for out-of-towners. There is a 1 in 2 chance each evening that one of the locals will seek a violent quarrel with the weakest-looking PC (i.e., the one with the lowest Strength ability score).

Such nuisances aside, St. Dagon Cove's proximity to the Temple by the Sea makes *The Spoiled Mermaid* an inexpensive refuge where battered adventurers can tend their wounds. Also, *The Spoiled Mermaid* is the only place in town where PCs can find mercenaries for hire (at a cost of 2 gp per day). Each night 0-3 (1d4-1) such mercenaries, each level 1-3, will be in the tavern.

ADVENTURE HOOK: LONG JOHN AHAB'S TALE OF WOE

While staying at the *Spoiled Mermaid*, the party is approached by **Long John Ahab**, a retired captain of a whaling ship. Long John Ahab is a salty old sea dog with a wooden leg and a chicken on his shoulder. In role-playing Ahab, the GM should feel free to improvise his or her best pirate speech.

Ahab offers the party a free round, and after a few pleasantries pulls up a chair and tells his tale of woe:

"A few miles up the coast from here stands the Dark Temple. It were built ages ago by those who adored the Old Sea God. Perhaps you never heard of the Old Sea God, but for hundreds of years he were the only god worshiped by men in these parts."

"The Old Sea God ain't worshiped no more, and a part of that is due to the Goblin Wars. Goblins came down here and put everyone to the sword, even the priests."

"But then the goblins all went mad and killed each other. So the temple were abandoned for a long time. That is, until Gregory Charcoal-burner come along."

At this point in the story, Long John Ahab pauses to spit on the floor before continuing.

"Gregory was nothin' to folks round here. No one thought anything of him. But one day he puts on airs, sayin' he had a revelation. Next thing you know, he's puttin' on airs and callin' himself "Zewlac" or some-such nonsense."

"I wouldn't care about none of this, but the scoundrel started talkin' to the folks in village, tryin' to get them to follow him and move into the old abandoned temple. Like he were God or somethin'! And a lot did follow him up there..."

"His followers, well they was mostly fools and layabouts, but then he starts charmin' some of the lady-folk. Charmin' ... bewitchin' them more like!"

At this point, Ahab pauses again, this time to down the remainder of his tankard. He then continues, with tears welling up in his eyes:

"And one of them lady-folk were my darlin' Elinor. Elinor... you never saw a more beautiful lass. But she were bewitched like the others. And now she's up there, with him."

Ahab pauses, this time to fish something from his pocket. He withdraws a single large coin and slams it on the table.

"That's one platinum piece. I've got 99 more for some brave folks who will march up to that temple and rescue my Elinor!"

"True, I had been feastin' a bit much the day she left, what with my nephew's birthday and all, and true it did take me three days before I knew she were gone. But when I did.... [Ahab begins crying] I didn't know what to do."

"I curse that Gregory, or Zewlac, or whatever he calls himself now! I only want my darlin' wife back. I'm a rich man, and will pay well if you bring her back to me. And mark my words, she is bewitched or she would not be up there with those people."

After one final pause, he exclaims in a loud voice "Elinor!" and slams his face on the table, sobbing. This draws several stares from neighboring tables.

Long John Ahab's long career was a violent one, and if pressed he is an accomplished fighter. In fact, he's capable of getting Elinor back himself but doesn't want the inconvenience of hiking several miles of rugged coastline with a wooden leg. Also, he and everyone else in St. Dagon's Cove have heard rumors of powerful, sinister beings in the temple (he'll keep this information to himself, but the PCs may hear it from other villagers). While Long John Ahab is fond of Elinor, in truth it's his pride that's hurt most of all. But he will not risk his life for his wife or his pride.

If the players accept the mission, Ahab will give them directions to the temple, but also tells them that the "weirdos" in the village square will likely take them to the temple if asked. Ahab will reassure the PCs that he doesn't think the cultists look very tough, though one should always be careful.

Ahab's chicken is trained to perch on his shoulder but nothing else, and will typically flee from combat.

Long John Ahab, Human Fighter 7: AC 13,
#At 1 cutlass, Dam 1d6+1, Mv 20', Ml 9, XP 800
STR 13 (+1), WIS 14 (+1), CON 16 (+2)

Equipment: **Cutlass +1**, leather armor, **Earrings of Spell Turning** (acts as a **Ring of Spell Turning** but the left earring holds 5 charges and the right holds 6). His wooden leg is hollow and contains a map to a tree under which he has buried a treasure chest with 372 pp, 1,287 gp, 40 ep, 899 sp, and 490 cp.

HP 44 ☐☐☐☐☐ ☐☐☐☐☐ ☐☐☐☐☐ ☐☐☐☐☐
☐☐☐☐☐ ☐☐☐☐☐ ☐☐☐☐☐ ☐☐☐☐☐
☐☐☐☐

Long John Ahab's Shoulder Chicken: AC 11,
HD 1d2 HP, #At 1 beak, Dam 1d2,
Mv 10' Fly 15'(10'), Sv NM, Ml 3, XP 10

HP 2 ☐☐

EQUIPMENT PURCHASES

St. Dagon's Cove features a smithy and general store where PCs can buy and sell items costing no more than 200 gp. To buy or sell more expensive items the party must travel 20 miles to the nearest large town.

VILLAGE SQUARE

The open space at the center of St. Dagon's Cove is rather small. Around its borders are numerous row houses, a small temple, a smithy, and a general store.

None of the locals appear to be spending much time in the square, with the notable exception of a young man and woman. These two wear identical brown robes and capes. Both have sandy blond hair and could be related. They would be attractive, though their appearance is marred by unkempt hair, noticeable dirt on their hands and bare feet and, as one approaches, the unmistakable scent of body odor.

The man and woman in brown are preaching. They are quite loud, and you catch phrases such as "Salvation" "Lord Zewlac", and "Open your minds, friends!". They are completely ignored by the locals, except for a couple boys standing some distance away making jokes.

If approached, these Zewlac-cultists will seize the occasion to discuss the group's core beliefs (see "The Zewlac Cult" below). With wide eyes they will

claim that Zewlac has brought them limitless peace, and that the only way to truly understand Zewlac and his teachings is to attend the "Ceremony", a ritual held every evening at the Dark Temple a few miles from town. If the party expresses an interest in attending the Ceremony or seeing Zewlac for themselves, the cultists offer to immediately accompany them on the short trek from village to temple.

The cultists have no possessions aside from their clothes, their daggers, and a copy of a book entitled *The Teachings of Zewlac*, which they will gladly give to potential converts. *The Teachings of Zewlac* is 80 pages of meandering parables, terrible love poetry, and illustrations of insect anatomy.

2 Zewlac-cultists: AC 9, HD 1d6 Hit Points, #At 1 dagger, Dam 1d4+2, Mv 40', Sv F1, Ml 11, XP 14 ea.

HP 5 ☐☐☐☐☐   4 ☐☐☐☐

These and other Zewlac-cultists fly into a rage whenever they believe their cult is under threat. This rage gives them a -2 to AC and a +2 to any damage rolls.

The Zewlac Cult

Any conversation with a Zewlac-cultist will cover any or all of the group's core beliefs:

1. Zewlac was once a normal man but through a miraculous revelation has become a perfect being.

2. Blind obedience to Zewlac is the only way to truly attain inner peace.

3. Work is unnecessary, unless following the orders of Zewlac.

4. Material possessions are unnecessary and should all be given to Zewlac to help spread his message.

5. Personal hygiene is unnecessary, and bathing is a cardinal sin.

6. It is forbidden to eat anything with more legs than oneself.

7. The meaning of life is to achieve Oneness with Zewlac. This is achieved through a ritual called the Ceremony, which is performed at the Dark Temple.

Each Zewlac-cultist is full of missionary zeal and will repeatedly stress the importance of the Ceremony to truly understand life, the universe, and everything.

If questioned about Long John Ahab's wife Elinor, Zewlac-cultists will speak glowingly of her goodness and generosity but profess ignorance about her current whereabouts ("oh she's in the temple somewhere", or "perhaps she stepped out to pick flowers"). In fact, the cultists are all aware that she was displeased with Zewlac and then, fearing for her life, fled to the temple's lower level and has not been seen since.

If Zewlac is killed, the cultists will disbelieve it unless shown proof. If they know Zewlac is dead, each cultist must make a morale check; success means they fly into a rage against Zewlac's killer, failure means they leave the temple complex to consider their life choices.

Travel from St. Dagon's Cove to the Dark Temple

A three-mile-long, rocky, winding trail leads directly from St. Dagon's Cove to the Dark Temple. The distance is short enough, and the region settled enough, that the trip should be uneventful and free of wandering monster encounters.

Temple Upper Level Key

As displayed in the maps, the temple has three levels and can only be entered via the upper level. The cultists are mostly confined to the upper level, the middle level is where Zewlac resides and performs secret rituals, and the lower level is inhabited by creatures loyal to the Old Sea God.

1. PORTICO:

> At the temple entrance are marble stairs leading to the wide temple door. To either side of the stairs is a curved row of seven pillars. As you approach the temple, two stern looking men in leather armor holding pikes glare at you.

If the party is accompanied by trusted cultists (e.g., from the village square in St. Dagon's Cove), the guards allow them to enter. Otherwise the guards will order them to leave or be attacked.

Sounds of battle from this area will lead Brother Kindar (room 2) to open the entry doors a crack and quickly peak out, after which he will shut and bar the doors and raise the alarm inside the temple. If this occurs, 1d4+2 rounds later the canein unit from room 8 will fling open the double doors and join the fray, and the following round the guards from room 12 will also join. Meanwhile, Brother Kindar will be going down to the middle level to warn and protect Zewlac.

Each guard has leather armor, a pike (polearm), a shortsword, and 2 gp. One guard has in his pocket a purported holy relic: the dried ear of St. Gertrude the Wholesome. It's not magical but will fetch 2 gp from any religious shopkeeper.

2 Guards, Human Fighter 1: AC 13, HD 1,
#At 1 polearm, Dam 1d10, Mv 40', Ml 8, XP 25 ea.
HP 7 ☐☐☐☐☐ ☐☐   7 ☐☐☐☐☐ ☐☐

2. FOYER:

> Beyond the temple entrance a chamber prominently features a basin for performing ablutions, now cracked and empty. Two dozen brown robes of various sizes lay in a pile in the corner of the room. The roof has a few holes but is mostly intact.

If the party is entering the temple peacefully, they are greeted here by Brother Kindar, Zewlac's trusted lieutenant:

> A tall, handsome middle-aged man wearing a filthy brown cape and robe smeared with grease approaches you. With a wide grin and arms outstretched, he exclaims "Welcome fellow-voyagers! I am brother Kindar, and I will be your guide".

Brother Kindar will give brown robes to visitors. Visitors may keep their weapons and armor ("we're all friends here") but must wear the robe over any armor.

Visitors wearing robes but not the capes worn by the cultists are known as "the wingless". Brother Kindar will spend a few minutes going over the group's beliefs (see "The Zewlac Cult" above) and then accompany them to the Common Room (room 4). Until the time of the communal supper at sundown visitors may remain in the Common Room or wander freely anywhere on the upper level.

Brother Kindar is a 3rd-level former Cleric who has been stripped of his spells after joining the Zewlac cult. As with all Zewlac-cultists defending their faith, in combat Kindar is filled with a wild rage that gives him -2 AC and +2 damage. Further, he carries a **Mace +1** and a **Scarab of Protection** (5 charges).

Brother Kindar, Human Cleric 3: AC 9,
#At 1 **mace +1**, Dam 1d6+3, Mv 40', MI 11, XP 145
HP 12 ☐☐☐☐☐ ☐☐☐☐☐ ☐☐

3. CULTIST SLEEPING QUARTERS:

> This room is crammed with eight bunk beds. Aside from the beds and a large fireplace it is empty.

This room is empty most of the time. Only from the end of the Ceremony until dawn do the cultists described in rooms 4 and 5 come here to sleep.

4. CULTIST COMMON ROOM:

> You are hit with an unwholesome smell of mother's home cooking mixed with body odor. Two 20-foot long tables and a large fireplace make this an ideal for communal meals.

This area is where cultists spend their leisure time while awaiting the evening's Ceremony. The room is occupied by filthy-but-cheerful cultists of all ages from dawn until the end of the evening communal supper, at which point they go to room 14 to attend the evening's Ceremony.

The communal supper is held at dusk and is open to visitors. The cultists here will greet visitors warmly provided there's no overt hostility.

During supper the cooks enter from the kitchen (room 5) and serve up dishes of piping hot stew with flagons of poor-quality wine. The meat in the stew appears to be pork, but if asked the cultists will claim it's chicken. In fact, it is human flesh. Anyone consuming it has a 1 in 6 chance of happening upon a finger or toe that will alert them to this.

If fighting breaks out, the cultists will swarm the party, their eyes blazing, their mouths foaming, and their knives waving wildly.

11 Zewlac-cultists: AC 9, HD 1d6 HP, #At 1 dagger, Dam 1d4+2, Mv 40', Sv NM, MI 11, XP 14 ea.

HP	1 ☐	4 ☐☐☐☐
	2 ☐☐	2 ☐☐
	3 ☐☐☐	3 ☐☐☐
	1 ☐	5 ☐☐☐☐☐
	1 ☐	6 ☐☐☐☐☐ ☐
	5 ☐☐☐☐☐	

5. KITCHEN:

> Obviously a kitchen, this room features a large fireplace, table, and three cupboards full of pots, pans, ladles, knives, bowls, and eating utensils. Two cheerful cultists are busy preparing a stew of beans, toasted cheese, and chunks of nondescript meat.

If the PCs inspect the "nondescript meat" closely they will discover it to be human flesh (leftovers from the previous night's Ceremony).

In the event of combat, the cooks are both armed with knives and frying pans.

2 Cultist Cooks: AC 9, HD 1d6 HP, #At 1 knife or frying pan, Dam 1d4+2, Mv 40', Sv F1, MI 11, XP 14 ea.

HP	6 ☐☐☐☐☐ ☐	4 ☐☐☐☐

6. PASSAGE TO MIDDLE LEVEL:

The door leading to this passage from the south has been reinforced with steel and is typically barred from the north side. Only Zewlac, Brother Kindar, the Three Sisters, or anyone in their company will gain entrance. No cultist is permitted to the middle level without Zewlac's permission, and no cultist ever descends to the lower level.

If the PCs gain entrance peacefully:

> Two cultists stand at the top of a flight of stairs that lead underground. These cultists wear the same brown capes as other Zewlac-cultists, but instead of the customary brown robes are instead clad in chain mail and armed with hand axes.

If they are attacked, one cultist will throw his hand ax at an enemy and then run down the stairs to the middle level to warn and protect Zewlac. The other will smash a vial of oil at the feet of the intruders before setting it alight. He has no regard for his personal safety, and would be happy if everyone in the room, including himself, was consumed by burning oil.

2 Zewlac-cultist guards: AC 13, HD 1d6 HP, #At 1 hand ax or flaming oil, Dam 1d6+2 or flaming oil, Mv 40', Sv F1, Ml 11, XP 14 ea.

HP 6 ☐☐☐☐☐ ☐   3 ☐☐☐

7. STOREROOM:

> Crates, bags, and shelves full of supplies fill this room to the brim. There is a faint smell of something rotting, containers are stacked haphazardly, and overall the room shows poor organization.

Most of the inventory in the storeroom are dry goods, including root vegetables, dried beans, flour, and salt. The storeroom's other contents include:

- 34 bottles of poor-quality wine (value 5 sp/bottle)
- 21 brown robes, each with a matching brown cape
- 9 wool blankets
- 2 lengths of rope (50' each)
- 1 hand ax
- 5 daggers
- 1 shortsword
- 2 suits of leather armor
- 1 suit of chain mail armor
- 1 teapot
- 220 nails (iron)
- 2 hammers
- 3 shovels
- 1 pick axe
- 2 chisels
- 1 bucket
- 1 roll of twine string (100')
- 8 flasks of oil
- 4 lanterns
- 1 ladder (8')

8. CANEIN UNIT:

> You are hit by a familiar smell... wet dog? A trio of large mastiff dogs are sitting on the floor. Sitting around them are three humanoids who also have mastiff faces.
>
> When you open the door all six look up and in unison mutter "woof!".

This room is an apartment for three canein mercenaries and their war dogs. The cult uses this team to retrieve would-be escapees. During combat the dogs bite and hold their target while the caneins use clubs to subdue and nets to ensnare. If alerted to trouble in area 1 they'll be on the scene in 1d4+2 rounds.

Each canein wears canein-fitted leather armor and carries a club and net. Their room features several straw mattresses, a chamber pot, medium-sized chest, night table, and lamp. The chest has a simple lock and contains 16 gp, 120 sp, and 80 cp.

3 Caneins: AC 14, HD 1, #At 1 bite, cudgel, or net, Dam 1d4 or 1d4 subdual, Mv 40', Sv F1 (+2 vs. Poison or Death Ray and Paralysis or Petrification), Ml 8, XP 25 ea.

HP 7 ☐☐☐☐☐ ☐☐   4 ☐☐☐☐
      8 ☐☐☐☐☐ ☐☐☐

3 Dogs: AC 14, HD 1+1, #At 1 bite, Dam 1d4 + hold, Mv 50', Sv F1, Ml 9, XP 25 ea.

HP 4 ☐☐☐☐   3 ☐☐☐
      8 ☐☐☐☐☐ ☐☐☐

9. THREE SISTERS' QUARTERS:

> Very spartan, even by the cultists' standards, this room only has three single beds and three simple wooden chairs in it.

This is the dwelling quarters of three females who assist in the cult's rituals. They never leave this chamber except for when they are called to participate in the Ceremony or the Transfiguration ritual.

They all share similar facial features and the same long hair, though the first two are auburn and the third white. They are significantly different in age: the first "sister" is a child of perhaps 12 years old, the second is a woman in her 30s, and the third is elderly. Their robes, unlike those of the cultists, are hooded and colored: the child's robe is white, the adult woman's red, and the old woman's black.

There is nothing of value in the room.

3 Cultists: AC 9, HD 1d6 HP, #At 1 dagger, Dam 1d4+2, Mv 40', Sv F1, Ml 11, XP 14 ea.

HP 1 ☐   4 ☐☐☐☐
      1 ☐

10. GOBLIN AMBASSADOR'S GUEST APARTMENT:

> This room is more luxurious than any other room you've seen in the temple. The room is dominated by a king-sized four poster bed made of polished oak and covered with silk sheets. All of the furniture is made of matching oak, including a dresser, a chair and small writing desk, and a large wardrobe standing in the corner.
>
> Sitting upon the bed are a small male goblin and a large female bugbear. The goblin is dressed in silk pantaloons, a velvet coat trimmed with (domestic) cat fur, a broad-brimmed feathered cap, and pair of lizardskin boots. The female bugbear wears a wolf-skin bikini. The goblin whispers something in the bugbear's ear and she lets out a boisterous laugh.

This room serves as the quarters of Toadthatch, the goblin ambassador to the temple. Toadthatch, along with his bugbear mistress Izolde, has been living on the cult's largess for several days. Zewlac has sought an alliance with the local goblin tribe to provide protection against interference by the local authorities, but both sides are still haggling over terms of payment.

Toadthatch is no fighter and won't hesitate to strike a deal to save his miserable hide. Izolde is made of braver stuff and will fight to defend true love.

Toadthatch's clothing is collectively worth 6 gp. In battle he wields a silver-bladed shortsword (value 60 gp). In the dresser is a small belt pouch with 8 gp and 11 ep. The wardrobe and dresser contain garish but well-made clothing worth a total of 5 gp and three garnets worth 10 gp each. Under the bed Toadthatch keeps three small sacks of walking around money: 20 gp, 20 sp, and 20 cp respectively.

Izolde wears a wolf-fur bikini and a gold necklace with an inset jade stone worth 130 gp.

Toadthatch: AC 11, HD 1-1, #At 1 shortsword, Dam 1d6, Mv 30', Sv F1, MI 7, XP 10

HP   4   ☐☐☐☐

Izolde: AC 13, HD 3+1, #At 1 longsword, Dam 1d8+1, Mv 40', Sv F3, MI 9, XP 145

HP   8   ☐☐☐☐☐ ☐☐☐

11. EMPTY GUEST APARTMENT:

> You see only a pair of double beds, a night stand, chamber pot, and two lamps.

This is where the party will be led if they pass themselves off as visiting potential converts.

12. BARRACKS:

> The room is furnished with a pair of single bunk beds, a pair of wardrobes, a pair of chests, and a lamp.

This room is where guards stationed in area 1 stay when they're off-duty. Typically there are always two on-duty guards in area 1 and two off-duty guards here.

If there's trouble the off-duty guards can quickly grab their shortswords, but in an emergency they won't take the time to don their leather armor.

The only things of worth in the room are two sets of leather armor in one of the wardrobes. The chests are full of clothing and personal effects, including a small belt pouch holding 5 gp, 3 sp, and 6 cp.

Each guard carries 2 gp and a shortsword.

2 Guards, Human Fighter 1: AC 11, HD 1, #At 1 shortsword, Dam 1d6, Mv 40', MI 8, XP 25 ea.

HP   2   ☐☐   8   ☐☐☐☐☐ ☐☐☐

13. BROTHER KINDAR'S QUARTERS:

> This room is obviously someone's living quarters, though its odd shape makes it only suitable for a single bed, one nightstand, and a lamp.

This is Brother Kindar's quarters, but he's only here at night between the time the Ceremony ends and dawn the next morning.

See room 2 for Brother Kindar's description and stats.

14. SANCTUARY:

> The temple's sanctuary is still usable, though in a state of disrepair. One section of the wall has completely collapsed so that it and the roof above are exposed to the open sky. Each side of the sanctuary is lined with a row of five pillars, but the pillar closest to the collapsed wall has toppled over and lays in sections on the floor.
>
> At the far end of the sanctuary sits an altar upon a raised dais.

The sanctuary is usually quiet and occupied by a single guard. Anyone could easily enter the chamber from outside the temple through the hole in the northwest wall, but would normally be observed by the guard who would raise the alarm.

Each night, about an hour after sunset the cult holds a ritual they call the Ceremony.

The Ceremony

The following text describes what happens if the characters are present during the Ceremony. At the start of the ritual, cultists from room 4 file into the sanctuary through the double doors and form a semi-circle surrounding the north-end dais. If the PCs are participating (willingly or unwillingly) in the Ceremony, they will also be told to form part of the semi-circle.

The Ceremony consists of 5 stages:

- A)   The Singing
- B)   The Master's Entrance
- C)   The Anointing
- D)   The First Revelation
- E)   The Second Revelation

A) The Singing:

> Once the congregation has formed a semi-circle around the alter, they begin spontaneously humming and gently rocking back and forth.

This goes on for about five minutes, during which time the humming gradually becomes louder and the rocking more energetic. The PCs are free to join in, but there is no issue if they choose not to.

B) The Master's Entrance:

> After the humming and rocking reaches a crescendo, someone cries out, "The Master approaches!"
>
> "The Master" is a small, unimpressive man. He has short, greasy hair, several days' beard growth, a long nose, and small beady black eyes that dart back and forth. He wears the same uniform as his followers: a dirty brown cassock and brown cape.
>
> Zewlac enters the chamber through the double doors, followed by three women. These women (the "Three Sisters", see room 9) are the only cultists who wear a different style of clothing: a long hooded robe. The robes of each woman are colored: the first (worn by a woman in her 30s) red, the second (worn by a young girl) is white, and the third (worn by an old woman) black. Each holds a small pot the size of a sugar bowl that's the same color as their robe.
>
> Zewlac and the three women slowly walk around one end of the semi-circle of cultists, stopping to face the person at one end.

C) The Anointing:

> Zewlac walks down the semi-circle of worshipers, staring searchingly into the eyes of each. After a moment's inspection, he tips his finger into one of the colored pots held by the Sisters and writes an X in colored dye upon the person's forehead.

The color of the dye has great significance. Upon placing it on the cultist, Zewlac will exclaim the appropriate italicized words below (i.e., "Blessed!", "Second Revelation!", or "Transfiguration!")

- **Red:** *Blessed.* Almost all of the congregation receive this mark, which doesn't really signify anything special.

- **White:** *Second Revelation.* Only one person per Ceremony receives this mark. It will typically be given to one of the regular cultists as a reward for their devotion (i.e., not a newcomer or captive).

- **Black:** *Transfiguration.* This honor is only rarely bestowed, but the GM may well see fit to have Zewlac apply the black mark to one of the PCs. When the black mark is applied, there are audible gasps and broad smiles among the congregation. If a PC is marked for Transfiguration, once the Ceremony is over the Three Sisters will escort him or her downstairs to the Preparation Chamber (room 16). If the Transfiguration candidate is willing, he or she may select one companion as a witness to accompany him or her through the ritual. If the person marked for Transfiguration is unwilling, Brother Kindar will summon the guards in room 6 and the canein unit in room 8 to coerce them. Party members not participating in the Transfiguration ritual may continue to wander freely on the temple's upper level.

D) The First Revelation:

> Standing behind the blood-stained alter, Zewlac exclaims in a loud voice: "What is the First Revelation?"
>
> With one voice, the congregation responds: "THE FORM OF ZEWLAC!"
>
> Suddenly, before your very eyes Zewlac's features change. His body darkens and becomes covered with a hard chitin, his eyes

grow large and black as coal, an extra set of arms extend out from his midsection, mandibles extend from his mouth, and antennas extend from the top of his head. At the end of this transformation Zewlac appears as a repulsive 6' tall insect: half man, half cockroach.

E) The Second Revelation:

Once Zewlac's transformation into roachman is complete, the candidate marked with the white X on their forehead quietly approaches the alter and lays upon it. They have a look of serene joy upon their face.

After a few moments, in a strange new, brittle voice, the roachman Zewlac asks, "What is the Second Revelation?"

To this, the congregation responds: "THE TASTE OF MAN-FLESH!"

Suddenly, with surprising agility Zewlac leaps upon the altar and begins devouring the candidate!

Once the candidate is dead and Zewlac has eaten his fill, Zewlac, remaining in hybrid form, will then exit through the East door and go back down to his underground lair (room 18).

Guard, Human Fighter 1: AC 13, HD 1, #At 1 longsword, Dam 1d8, Mv 40', MI 8, XP 25

HP 4 ☐☐☐☐

For stats of Ceremony attendees, see room 2 for Brother Kindar, room 4 for the cultists, room 9 for the Three Sisters, and room 18 for Zewlac.

Temple Middle Level Key

15. SACRED VERMIN:

The floors of this room are covered in rotting garbage and teeming with hundreds of roaches. A couple of these roaches are several feet in length.

The occupants of the room are 1 insect swarm and 2 giant cockroaches. These beings are considered holy by the cultists. The cockroaches can sense those who do not respect cockroaches and will deal with them accordingly.

Insect Swarm (mundane cockroaches): AC 13 (see Note below), HD 2*, #At 1 swarm, Dam 1d3 (double against no armor), Mv 10' Fly 20', Sv N/A, MI 11, XP 100

HP 7 ☐☐☐☐☐ ☐☐

Note: It is possible to "ward off" swarming cockroaches by swinging a weapon, shield, or other similar-sized object around, and in this case also damage is reduced to 1 point per round. If a lit torch is used in this way, the swarm takes 1d4 points of damage per round. Weapons, even magical ones, do not harm an insect swarm. An entire swarm can be affected by a **sleep** spell. Smoke can be used to drive a swarm away (if the swarm moves away from the victim(s) due to smoke, the damage stops immediately).

2 Giant Cockroaches: AC 15, HD 1*, #At 1 bite, Dam 1d4, Mv 50', Sv F1 (immune to disease, saves as C10 vs. Poison), MI 6, XP 37 ea.

HP 6 ☐☐☐☐☐ ☐   3 ☐☐☐

16. PREPARATION CHAMBER:

This room appears completely empty except for a large rectangular table in the middle and a medium-sized clay pot at its base.

This room is set aside to prepare for Zewlac's Transfiguration ceremony. Those who receive the black mark during the Ceremony (see room 14) are brought here by the 3 Sisters (stats in room 9). At all other times, the room is uninhabited.

Transfiguration Ritual Preparation

If a candidate is brought to the room in preparation for Transfiguration:

One of the Sisters asks you to undress completely and lay on the table. The table is of solid pine wood but otherwise unremarkable.

The Sisters then apply the contents of the pot – a dark brown ointment with a musky odor – to the candidate's body.

Once the ointment is applied, the Three Sisters will firmly instruct the naked candidate to remain in the room until Brother Kindar arrives. They leave the candidate's clothes and other belongings in a corner of the room, but lock the door on the east side behind them.

The door on the west side of the room remains unlocked but is a trap, a "test of faith" for those told to wait for the Transfiguration ritual. Anyone weighing over 50 lbs stepping on the floor west of the western door (area 16a) triggers the floor to open to a pit beneath them. The pit is 30' deep, causing 3d6 points of falling damage. The bottom of the pit is an empty 10' x 10' chamber adjacent to room 21 via a secret door.

If the candidate waits as instructed, after 30 minutes Brother Kindar arrives with the Three Sisters, unlocks the door, and accompanies the candidate down several flights of stairs and hallways to the Transfiguration Chamber (room 17).

17. TRANSFIGURATION CHAMBER:

> The doorway to this room opens to a short 10' long passageway leading to a 20' x 30' room. Above the entrance to the room from the passageway is a raised portcullis. A winch on the north side of the passageway is attached to chains running up to the ceiling, apparently the mechanism for raising and lowering the portcullis.
>
> The room itself is completely bare of furnishings.

A search for secret doors may reveal the trap door in the ceiling, but the ceiling is 10' above the floor and the room furnishes no means to access it.

Transfiguration Ritual Event

Those who receive a Black mark during the Ceremony (see room 14) are escorted by Brother Kindar and the Three Sisters to room 16, where they are prepared for the Transfiguration ritual. They are then brought here, to room 17, and told to wait while Brother Kindar lowers the portcullis. If the candidate is not willing, Brother Kindar may enlist the canein unit (room 8) or guards as backup.

If a PC is in the room awaiting Transfiguration:

> Suddenly, the silence of this underground chamber is broken by the unsettling sound of a large creature scurrying above you. The sound gradually gets louder until it's directly overhead and then stops. You hear a loud voice reverberating from somewhere above this room: *"There are many ways to become One with Zewlac!"*

> The voice is followed by the creaking of a door, and you see a trapdoor opening in the ceiling. (You hadn't noticed the trapdoor before, it must have been hidden.) Through the trapdoor emerges a pair of black insect-like antennae, at least a couple feet in length. Following the antennae is the grotesque face of a roachman: shiny black bug eyes, mandibles protruding from the mouth, and spikes sticking out of black insect-like limbs.

This is Zewlac a werecockroach in roachman form entering the chamber from room 18. As Zewlac enters the room he will transform into giant cockroach form and attack the victim with his bite attack. Zewlac's goal isn't to kill the victim but to infect him or her with lycanthropy (i.e, "Transfiguration"). So once the victim loses half or more of his or her hit points to Zewlac's bites, Zewlac breaks off the attack, returns to his lair through the trapdoor in the ceiling, and Brother Kindar raises the portcullis.

As with other forms of lycanthropy, an infected person will become a werecockroach in 3d6 days. Anyone thus infected is considered highly blessed and venerated by the cultists, though not to the point of being worshiped like Zewlac.

18. TOMB OF ST. DAGON (ZEWLAC'S LAIR):

Rooms 18, 20, and 21 were sections of the catacombs hidden away to entomb the arch-priests of the Old Sea God cult.

The first of these rooms (18), the Tomb of Saint Dagon, was the sepulcher of one of the senior followers of the Old Sea God. Zewlac has now adopted it as his lair.

While in this room, Zewlac remains in his roachman or giant roach form. He's almost always here except when he's conducting the Ceremony in room 14 or the Transfiguration ritual in room 17. For the latter, in roachman form he goes through the secret door on the east wall and from a 5' square pit in the floor crawls down a 40' chute into a 10' x10' room built atop the northwest corner of room 17 (though the chute has iron rungs for climbing up or down, the werecockroach doesn't need them). A trapdoor in the floor opens to room 17, where Zewlac will find the Transfiguration candidate (willing or unwilling).

There is a stone coffin in the center of room 18. The coffin's lid requires a combined strength of 30 to shove aside. The coffin is completely empty. On both sides of the coffin's base, are carved the words "REST IN PEACE SAINT DAGON".

In the corner of the room is a trunk with the treasure Zewlac has amassed from his followers: 362 gp, 1,354 sp, 2 **Potions of Healing**, and a jeweled belt (formerly Elinor's) worth 210 gp.

Zewlac (Werecockroach): AC 15†, HD 3**,
#At 1 bite, Dam 1d6, Mv 30' Fly 60' (10'), Sv F3*,
Ml 8, XP 205

HP 20 ☐☐☐☐☐ ☐☐☐☐☐ ☐☐☐☐☐ ☐☐☐☐☐

As a werecockroach, Zewlac can only be hit by silver or magic weapons, and saves as a Fighter 3 for everything except save as a Cleric 17 vs. Poison. Werecockroaches are immune to all non-magical diseases.

19. SURPRISE GHOUL ROACH:

Read this as the party passes through the hallway adjacent to the secret door:

> The walls in this hallway appear to have been recently plastered over. As you pass through, you distinctly hear a scratching noise that seems to come from the western wall.

The ghoul cockroach scratches the wall when it senses warm-blooded prey on the other side. Due to this noise, chances to discover this secret door are doubled.

When the secret door is opened the ghoul cockroach emerges to attack:

> Suddenly, a 3' long deathly white cockroach bursts onto the scene, its mandibles slicing the air with terrific speed and viciousness.

Giant Ghoul Cockroach: AC 16, HD 2**, #At 1 bite, Dam 1d6 bite +paralysis +disease, Mv 50', Sv F2 (C10 vs. Poison; immune to disease), Ml 12, XP 125

HP 10 ☐☐☐☐☐ ☐☐☐☐☐

Ghoul cockroaches can be Turned by a Cleric (as a ghoul).

20. TOMB OF ST. TRILLOD:

> This subterranean chamber features a large stone coffin in the center. On both sides of the coffin, at its base, are carved the words "REST IN PEACE SAINT TRILLOD".
>
> Several piles of blankets are stuffed on the edges of the room. Between that and the smell, this tomb is obviously now serving as someone's dwelling quarters.

This room holds the sepulcher of Saint Trillod, a holy woman who was a great friend to barnacles.

It has become the home of four cultists who want to prove their worth by remaining in the cold and dark. Like all other rooms on this level, the room is pitch black. The cultists will fight intruders with or without light.

The lid of the stone coffin requires a combined Strength of 30 to shove aside.

The skeleton in the coffin once wore costly robes, but age has rendered them threadbare and worthless. The skeleton clutches a silver-plated three-pronged trident (value 60 gp) (see the **Equipment Emporium** for a description of tridents).

4 Zewlac-cultists: AC 9, HD 1d6 Hit Points,
#At 1 dagger, Dam 1d4+2, Mv 40', Sv F1, Ml 11,
XP 14 ea.

HP 6 ☐☐☐☐☐ ☐   5 ☐☐☐☐☐
6 ☐☐☐☐☐ ☐   4 ☐☐☐☐

21. TOMB OF ST. SKURKIN:

> The door opens to a cold chamber devoid of any furnishings except a large stone coffin in the center. On both sides of the coffin, at its base, are carved the words "SAINT SKURKIN [Undecipherable] IN PEACE". The missing word has been destroyed roughly with a chisel.

This room holds another saint's tomb. It's identical to room 20 except that it's larger and features a secret door. The cultists generally leave this room unoccupied.

The lid of the stone coffin requires a combined Strength of 30 to shove aside. The skeleton wears a silver circlet and holds a silver-tipped spear (each worth 5 gp).

The area beyond the secret door on the east side is 30' below the covered pit in room 16A.

Temple Lower Level Key

Unlike the upper level and middle level, the lower level is completely avoided by the Zewlac cult. This level was originally the most sacred part of the Old Sea God's temple, where the most sacred rituals were performed. When the temple was conquered during the Goblin Wars, at first the invading hobgoblins left the lower level alone out of deference to alien gods they didn't understand. But the hobgoblin chieftain was greedy, and after hearing rumors of great wealth in the vaults beneath the temple, he personally led a band to loot it.

This decision proved fatal to the chieftain and his soldiers, for the Old Sea God took vengeance through a powerful curse. Two malevolent spirits took possession of the two greatest hobgoblin warriors, who single-highhandedly slew the chieftain and most of the contingent. The carnage only stopped when hobgoblin shamans were able to place protective wards in room 22 that prevented the evil from spreading to the middle and upper levels.

The hobgoblin invaders have long since gone, but the curse remains in effect throughout the lower level, which is still warded off from the rest of the complex. Although worshipers no longer visit the

place, several rooms have been magically restored to the state they were in back in the heyday of the Old Sea God. In these places dwell luminescent light, pool, and aquatic creatures eager to slay all who will not kneel before the Old Sea God.

22. THE BLACK DOOR:

> The room is empty and unoccupied. The wooden door on the west wall has been painted black. In the center of the door a 3' diameter circular design has been carved into the wood. The carving is so deep that its design appears in bright contrast to the black door.

To any players who know the goblin language:

> You instantly recognize that the engravings are of goblin – or more specifically, hobgoblin – origin. The symbols are of an arcane nature and are mostly too obscure to translate. But you do clearly recognize markings that signify "DEMON", "MADNESS", and "FORBIDDEN".

To any players who are Magic-Users:

> You recognize that the engravings are related to goblin shamanistic banishment rituals. But their precise meaning is undecipherable.

The door is unlocked, but the circular carving is a magical ward put in place by hobgoblin shamans. As long as the ward exists, none of the creatures from the lower level may enter room 22 or the levels above. When such creatures try to move through the doorway they experience the equivalent of an invisible **wall of iron** and take 1d6 points of damage each round he or she spends in the doorway or (were it possible) beyond.

Though the design channels powerful magic, the physical carving itself is non-magical. If the carving is destroyed (e.g., by scraping it off with a chisel or bladed instruments), the ward disappears and all lower level denizens–most notably the two odeums in rooms 27 and 31–would be released from their imprisonment.

23. HAUNTED, MUTINOUS BONES:

This 20' x 20' room once held a 15' diameter, 3' deep pool in its center. The pool's water has long since disappeared. The pool only contains the skeleton of a single hobgoblin.

As soon as you enter the room, the skeleton quickly jumps up and begins swinging a morning star over its head.

In life this hobgoblin had been a commander, but under the influence of malicious temple spirits took part in a mutiny against his chieftain. After the final battle in which most of the hobgoblins were slain (see room 26) he came to this room with a sack of loot but later died of his wounds.

The haunted bones skeleton is armed with a **Morningstar +1**. Nearby is a large bag containing 4 cp, 353 sp, 301 gp, and 9 pp.

Haunted Bones Skeleton: AC 15, HD 3, #At 1 morning star, Dam 1d8+1, Mv 50', Sv F3, Ml 12, XP 145

HP 13 ☐☐☐☐☐ ☐☐☐☐☐ ☐☐☐

Like an ordinary skeleton, a haunted bones skeleton takes only half damage from edged weapons, and only a single point from arrows, bolts, and sling stones (plus any magical bonus). As with all undead, it can be Turned by a Cleric (as a ghoul), and is immune to **sleep**, **charm**, and **hold** spells.

24. STORAGE CLOSET:

This was once a storage room, stuffed with boxes and sacks. Most are rotting, and from the caked dust and musty smell it's obvious the room is no longer in use.

A pair of highly territorial vort snakes have made this room their residence, and will attack any intruders.

2 Vort Snakes: AC 15, HD 1+2, #At 1 bite, Dam 1d3 + poison, Mv 50', Sv as F1, Ml 7, XP 25 ea.

HP 6 ☐☐☐☐☐ ☐
     7 ☐☐☐☐☐ ☐☐

The poison of the vort snake is only lethal to small-sized (e.g., Halfling) creatures, for whom a failed save vs. Poison results in death. Medium or larger-sized creatures who fail their saving throw are rendered unconscious for 2d4 turns.

25. ARCH-PRIEST'S APARTMENT:

You see several piles of broken, rotting furniture. It looks like this might have been a living suite for a high-ranking person, but everything has been ruined beyond repair.

The only thing of note is a skeleton laying upon debris that might have once been a bed. The skeleton has a javelin thrust through its sternum.

This was originally the room of the arch-priest. It has been thoroughly looted and vandalized by hobgoblins.

If the party find the secret door to area 27, they will see a small compartment in the secret door's frame. That compartment has 1 **Wand of Lightning Bolts** (4 charges).

26. SIGNS OF BATTLE:

This 20' x 20' room was the site of a violent skirmish. At least a dozen skeletons are sprawled on the ground, all of which appear to be hobgoblin. All skeletons are armed with spears, a few positioned so they're still piercing their fellow hobgoblins.

Two of the hobgoblin corpses are undead haunted bones skeletons. These belong to the hobgoblin chieftain and one of his rebellious lieutenants. These two were specially cursed by the Old Sea God to remain here after their deaths as permanent guardians to the temple's lower level.

The chieftain (20 HP) haunted bones has a **Dagger +1** strapped to his ankle and a gold ring with an inset jade stone worth 120 gp.

2 Haunted Bones Skeletons: AC 15, HD 3, #At 1 spear, Dam 1d8, Mv 50', Ml 12, Sv F3, XP 145 ea.

HP 20 ☐☐☐☐☐ ☐☐☐☐☐ ☐☐☐☐☐ ☐☐☐☐☐
      8 ☐☐☐☐☐ ☐☐☐

Like an ordinary skeleton, a haunted bones skeleton takes only half damage from edged weapons, and only a single point from arrows, bolts, and sling stones (plus any magical bonus). As with all undead, it can be Turned by a Cleric (as a ghoul), and is immune to **sleep**, **charm**, and **hold** spells.

27. HALL OF OBEISANCE AND SECRET SHRINE:

> The area behind the secret door leads to a 50' long hallway. Unlike other halls and rooms in this complex, the walls are completely unfinished, and large stalactites hang from the ceiling, which at 20' is higher than that of the chamber you just came from. This area appears to have been part of a natural cave network that existed for thousands of years before the original temple was built.

If the party begin walking down the hallway, a **magic mouth** appears on the wall next to them and speaks. Each person hears a message in their own native tongue:

> The magic mouth speaks in a booming voice that echos down the hall:
>
> "LAND-DWELLERS, SHOW OBEISANCE TO THE LORD OF THE OCEANS!"

Upon saying these words, the mouth disappears.

The spirit guardians of this place will acknowledge any act of deference as "obeisance" (e.g., bowing, words of supplication, etc.), and will leave such persons alone. On the other hand, any person who fails to show obeisance will be attacked by one of the eight darkmantles that appear to be stalactites on the ceiling.

Note that although there are eight darkmantles, only one will attack each person who fails to show obeisance.

The 10' x 10' area extending from the middle of the north side of the hallway is an alcove within which is a statue of the Old Sea God, decapitated in an act of blasphemous vandalism by hobgoblins. If the party reaches this area:

> When you reach the center of the hallway, a 10' x 10' alcove extends out of the corridor's north side. Within the alcove is an 8' stone statue of a humanoid with a crab claw in place of its right hand, tentacle in place of its left arm, and the form of a scaly fish below the waste. The statue's head has been roughly shorn off and is nowhere to be found.
>
> A coffer sits at the statue's feet, but any offerings it once held have been long since pilfered.

If anyone in the party touches the statue: a transparent bald woman in a flowing robe steps out of the statue. This is the spirit of St. Trillod, an odeum. St. Trillod will attack whomever touched the statue with wisdom-draining attacks and then attempt to take possession of them.

As with all undead, an odeum can be Turned by a Cleric (as a wraith), and is immune to **sleep**, **charm**, and **hold** spells. Odeums take damage from holy water, whether in corporeal form (e.g., possessing someone) or incorporeal form. The temple's lower level contains large reservoirs of holy water in rooms 30, 32, and 33.

If the statue is pushed over it will shatter. Within its chest is a black pearl worth 500 gp.

8 Darkmantles: AC 17, HD 1+2, #At 1 constriction, Dam 1d4, Mv 20' Fly 60', Sv F1, Ml 7, XP 37 ea.

HP	7 ▢▢▢▢▢ ▢▢	10 ▢▢▢▢▢ ▢▢▢▢▢
	8 ▢▢▢▢▢ ▢▢▢	10 ▢▢▢▢▢ ▢▢▢▢▢
	4 ▢▢▢▢	9 ▢▢▢▢▢ ▢▢▢▢
	4 ▢▢▢▢	6 ▢▢▢▢▢ ▢

St. Trillod (Odeum): AC 16 ⚔, HD 4, #At 1 touch, Dam 1d6 touch damage + 1d4 wisdom drain or possession, Mv 60' Fly, Sv F4, Ml 12, XP 280

HP 20 ▢▢▢▢▢ ▢▢▢▢▢ ▢▢▢▢▢ ▢▢▢▢▢

28. THE STATUE KNOWS:

> This trapezoidal chamber features two doors next to each other on the north wall. The door on the left is painted bright green; the door on the right is painted dark blue. Standing near the south wall directly facing the doors is a 15' tall dark lava-stone statue of a bald, robed female. Her left hand is placed on her stomach, her right hand raised at the elbow and pointing the index finger toward the ceiling.

The statue is actually a stone living statue. A few moments after the party enters the room it becomes animated:

> Suddenly, you hear a deep creaking noise coming from the statue. It slowly turns its face toward you and points toward a member of your party.

The statue will slowly, ponderously point at each member of the party and then point at one of the two colored doors. The GM should determine this randomly for character (d2: 1=green door, 2=blue door).

Once the statue has pointed each character toward a door it will return to its original position and inert state.

Regardless of whether a character decides to enter the colored door indicated for them by the statue, the statue doesn't enforce these directives or pose any threat to the party. It will, however, defend itself if attacked.

If the PCs do enter room 33 through either colored door, keep track of who enters which door. The significance of the two doors is explained in the room 33 description.

Living Statue, Stone: AC 16, HD 5*, #At 2 lava sprays, Dam 2d6/2d6, Mv 20', Sv F5, Ml 12, XP 405

HP 23 ☐☐☐☐☐ ☐☐☐☐☐ ☐☐☐☐☐ ☐☐☐☐☐
☐☐☐

29. ROOM OF SHELLS:

> For whatever reason, five huge piles of shells are spaced evenly around the floor. Each pile has a mix of various kinds: oysters, clams, mussels, etc.

There's nothing exceptional about the shells, and the original purpose of the room is unknown.

30. SACRED POOL OF CRUSTACEANS:

> This 20' x 20' room is dominated by a 15' diameter pool in its center. The pool extends 3' deep into the floor of the room. The water of the pool is luminescent, bathing the entire chamber in a cool blue light.
>
> The bottom of the pool is sandy and littered with glittering coins and precious stones. It is empty of living things, except for an enormous crab five feet across.
>
> Upon seeing your entrance, the crab ambles towards you, pincers outstretched.

There used to be other crabs and lobsters in this pool, but the giant crab ate them all (that's how it got to be giant). As a loyal subject of the Old Sea God, the crab will attack intruders.

The pool's light is created by the fact that it is magical, holy water. Clerics or paladins will recognize it as such.

Upon the pool bottom are 71 cp, 28 sp, 3 ep, 35 gp, 12 pp, and 7 semiprecious stones worth 50 gp each.

Giant Crab: AC 18, HD 3, #At 2 pincers,
Dam 2d6/2d6, Mv 20' Swim 20', Sv F3, Ml 7, XP 145

HP 14 ☐☐☐☐☐ ☐☐☐☐☐ ☐☐☐☐

31. MEDITATION CHAMBER (ELINOR):

> In the center of this tiny 10' x 10' completely bare nook, a woman in the brown uniform of the Zewlac-cult sits cross-legged, eyes closed.
>
> This woman has seen better days. Her robes are stained black with mud and dried blood. As the party enters, her eyes snap open.

Despite the placidity of her initial appearance, Elinor will interact normally with the party, expressing great gratitude at the prospect of being rescued. She is disenchanted with Zewlac

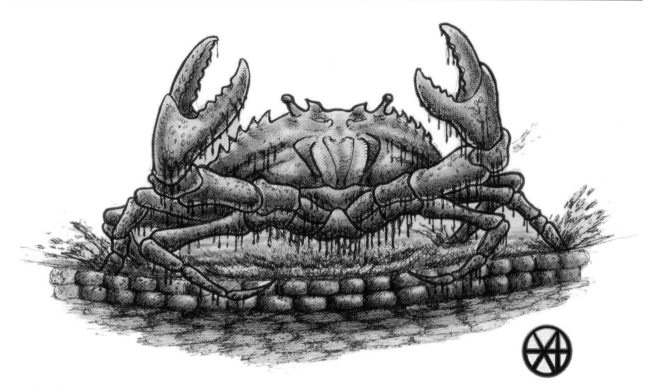

and claims she wishes to leave. If her estranged husband Long John Ahab is mentioned she will quickly change the subject.

Elinor is possessed by the spirit of St. Skurkin, an odeum set on destroying all nonbelievers who currently desecrate the temple with their presence.

As with the odeum in room 27, unless the protection glyphs in room 22 are removed neither the odeum nor any creature it possesses may pass through the doors between room 22 and the rest of the lower level. Thus, the goal of the odeum is not to immediately wipe out the party but rather to escape its imprisonment and then destroy both the party and the Zewlac-cultists.

To do this, "Elinor" will seek to convince the party that the magic ward on the door in room 22 was placed by the Zewlac-cultists to prevent Elinor's escape. She believes, correctly, that it can be scraped off the door and this will allow her to leave the Lower Level.

If this approach doesn't work or if the odeum is found out, the odeum will cause Elinor's suicide and then seek to possess a member of the party:

> From Elinor's lifeless body floats a transparent figure. This figure doesn't look like Elinor, but instead is in the form of a wild-haired, bearded older man in flowing robes.

In possessing a member of the party, the odeum will seek to influence the party any way it can to remove the magic ward (e.g., through persuasion or threats to end its new host's life through suicide).

As with all undead, an odeum can be Turned by a Cleric (as a wraith), and is immune to **sleep**, **charm**, and **hold** spells. Odeums take damage from holy water, whether in corporeal form (e.g., possessing Elinor) or incorporeal form. The temple's lower level contains large reservoirs of holy water in rooms 30, 32, and 33.

Elinor: AC 11, HD 1d4 HP, #At 1 dagger, Dam 1d4, Mv 40', Sv NM, Ml 12, XP 10

HP   4   ☐☐☐☐

St. Skurkin (Odeum): AC 16†, HD 4, #At 1 touch, Dam 1d6 touch damage + 1d4 wisdom drain or possession, Mv 60' Fly, Sv F4, Ml 12, XP 280

HP   19   ☐☐☐☐☐ ☐☐☐☐☐ ☐☐☐☐☐ ☐☐☐☐

32. SACRED POOL OF FISH:

This 20' x 20' room is dominated by a 15' diameter pool in its center. The pool extends 3' deep into the floor of the room and teems with beautiful multicolored fish of various sizes. The water of the pool is somehow luminescent, bathing the entire chamber in a cool blue light.

The pool's light is created by the fact that it is magical, holy water. Clerics or paladins will recognize it as such. There is nothing exceptional or dangerous about the fish in the pool. The bottom of the pool used to be covered in offerings of precious coins and stones, but these were looted by the hobgoblins.

33. POOL OF OFFERING AND SACRIFICE:

Those entering this chamber from room 28 do so either through a green door or a blue door (see room 28). The two identical passageways leading from these doors are separated by a wall.

The colored door leads to a 10' wide passageway which leads to a 20' long run of steps. As you begin going down the stairs, you can see ahead the passageway opens up to a large chamber, illuminated by a pale blue light. This chamber is flooded, and about 5' from the chamber entrance the steps become submerged. Judging by where the water level starts on the stairs in relation to the room, the water level in the room appears about 3' deep.

In fact, the water is 3' deep near the southern entrance, but 20' from the entrance there are two more downward steps, making the northern 2/3 of the chamber 4' deep.

The chamber is roughly oval-shaped and about 70' long and 40' wide (much larger than any of the other rooms you've seen in the temple's lower levels).

On either side of the room are wide columns. Columns, walls, and, ceiling are covered in thousands of polished blue and green ceramic tiles.

The water itself provides a glowing blue illumination, perhaps by magic. It is surprisingly clear, and on the bottom you catch the glint of hundreds of coins and shiny stones.

When the temple was in the service of the Old Sea God, some worshipers would enter the blue door with offerings of coins and gems and others would enter the green door with living sacrifices of livestock. For hundreds of years, generations of sacred eels living in this pool learned that anything coming through the green door (see room 28) was food. Those entering via the passageway leading from the green door will instantly be savagely attacked by 13 eels. Those emerging from the blue door passageway will be left alone.

The pool's light is created by the fact that it is magical, holy water. Clerics or paladins will recognize it as such.

The following treasure is underwater on the chamber floor: 2,927 sp, 1,431 gp, 67 pp, 41 moss agate (10 gp each), 17 lapis lazuli (20 gp each), and 3 pearls (100 gp each).

13 Eels: AC 11, HD 1, #At 1 bite, Dam 1d6, Mv 60' Swim, Sv F1, Ml 8, XP 25 ea.

HP	7 ☐☐☐☐☐ ☐☐	7 ☐☐☐☐☐ ☐☐
	3 ☐☐☐	2 ☐☐
	2 ☐☐	4 ☐☐☐☐
	6 ☐☐☐☐☐ ☐	2 ☐☐
	6 ☐☐☐☐☐ ☐	1 ☐
	4 ☐☐☐☐	2 ☐☐
	4 ☐☐☐☐	

Ending the Adventure

Long John Ahab is as good as his word, and will give the party the remaining 99 pp upon Elinor's return. Perversely, he will even deliver the reward if Elinor's corpse is returned to him.

If the GM wishes, there are several possibilities for follow-on adventures:

- Elinor must have been pretty unhappy in her marriage to have chosen a cult of cockroach-worshipers over life with her husband. For this reason, she'll fight tooth-and-nail against a return home. You may complicate the situation further by having Elinor fall in love with one of the PCs.

- If one or both of the odeums are released they will seek new hosts, perhaps powerful locals (e.g., Long John Ahab)

- The third saint of the Old Sea God, "Saint Dagon," is unaccounted for.

- Not all of the Zewlac-cultists dwelt at the temple. Those who remain may seek vengeance, perhaps under a new leader.

The Horror Within
by Russ Robinson

The Hook

The party's cleric(s) have been summoned by their deity's high priest, Jorak, in his cathedral at Slateholm. A young priest of the order named Tarn recently led a group of acolytes to reclaim an ancient temple, but the church feels they were unprepared for the task and may be in danger. The church would look favorably upon the party traveling to the temple to join them. Jorak expects the party's clerics to accept the mission without promise of reward but is prepared to outfit a beginning group of adventurers with up to 300 gp worth of equipment and will give each cleric a **Potion of Healing** as they set out.

What's Really Going On?

After the hobgoblins were driven from the sea god's temple, malevolent priests used the remote location to perform wicked and unholy experiments, releasing undead upon the neighboring lands. A righteous crusade descended upon the temple and cleared it of all but the most powerful evil, which they sealed into the lowest level with powerful holy magic.

That was more than a century ago, and now in addition to Tarn's acolytes, the temple is being explored by 2 bands of nefarious marauders in hopes of claiming it as a fortress, as well as sacking any riches that might still lay within.

The first is a band of goblins led by a hobgoblin; they have managed to make their way to the lower levels of the temple but are finding the traps and undead to be much more than they bargained for.

The second is a band of evil adventurers led by the unholy cleric Nebi, who have recently arrived and are gleefully dispatching Tarn and his unprepared holy men as well as the overwhelmed goblins.

Room 33 in the lowest level of the temple is sealed and may not be entered until the **2 golden disks** (found in areas 17 and 27) are placed into the door in order to break the seal. Room 27 may not be entered until the **3 keys** (found in areas 5, 16a, and 30) are turned in the key holes in areas 25, 26, and 32, exposing the secret doors. Room 33, the temple, contains The Horror Within are the original

evil high priests (now undead themselves) and their horrifying creation, the original hobgoblin chieftain they reanimated as a nauseatingly undead abomination. If the party fails to defeat the undead high priests or flees, they will begin animating any and all corpses within the temple and begin to again terrorize the land.

Getting To The Temple

If the party asks around and gathers information about the temple locally, they may discover a few rumors concerning it:

1. The wizard Nesa has disappeared in that area, along with her collection of exotic potions and elixirs.

2. I hear that a dragon has made that temple its lair

3. I came near that place once and will never do it again! I saw huge shapes circling in the sky above.

4. It's got a death curse! All who enter are cursed!

5. Goblins, ain't nothing but goblins up there. Ghosts ain't nothing but spook stories to scare children.

6. Everyone knows that old hobgoblin chief had a chest of gold and a magical axe but ain't nobody got nerve enough to go lookin' fer it.

The journey to the temple itself takes 6 days travel and will be uneventful other than unnerving events such as seeing large, dark shapes circling overhead, rustling and growling within the woods to wake the party in the night, and/or the half-consumed corpse of a horse with saddle stretched across the road. It is not suggested to weaken the party before they arrive at the temple as a low-level band of adventurers will require all their resources. However, if the players are dragging their feet, the GM should feel free to spur them along however he sees fit since there is a sense of urgency in finding Tarn and his crusaders.

The Arrival

> The rocky path along the seaside cliff you have been traveling abruptly ends at a copse of twisted trees and brambles. You find a recently made path through the hostile underbrush and follow it for half an hour before it opens to a clearing containing a large stone structure, impossibly perched upon the cliffside overhanging the sea. You breathe a short-lived sigh of relief at having reached the ancient and crumbling temple of the sea god, and then realize that your journey has only begun.

Wandering Monsters

On a roll of 1-2 on 1d6, roll for an encounter from the table below.

1. **1d4 Bandits** (12 total before being exhausted): AC 14, HD 1, #At 1, Dam 1d6, Mv 30', Sv F1, Ml 9, XP 25 ea.
   Equipment: leather armor, shield, short sword, 1d6 silver

HP	7 ☐☐☐☐☐ ☐☐	7 ☐☐☐☐☐ ☐☐
	6 ☐☐☐☐☐ ☐	6 ☐☐☐☐☐ ☐
	6 ☐☐☐☐☐ ☐	5 ☐☐☐☐☐
	5 ☐☐☐☐☐	5 ☐☐☐☐☐
	4 ☐☐☐☐	4 ☐☐☐☐
	3 ☐☐☐	2 ☐☐

2. **1d4 Goblins:** AC 14, HD 1-1, #At 1, Dam 1d6, Mv 20', Sv F1, Ml 7, XP 10 ea.
   Equipment: rusty short swords, 1d4 sp

HP	4 ☐☐☐☐	4 ☐☐☐☐
	3 ☐☐☐	2 ☐☐

3. **1d3 Dogs (as area #2):** AC 14, HD 1+1, #At 1+hold, Dam 1d4, Mv 50', Sv F1, Ml 9, XP 25 ea.

HP	6 ☐☐☐☐☐ ☐	5 ☐☐☐☐☐
	5 ☐☐☐☐☐	

4. **Evil Party from Room 13** (unless already defeated)

5. **1d3 Skeletons:** AC 13, HD 1, #At 1, Dam 1d6, Mv 40', Sv F1, Ml 12, XP 25 ea.

HP	6 ☐☐☐☐☐ ☐	5 ☐☐☐☐☐
	4 ☐☐☐☐	

6. **1d2 Giant Crab Spiders:** AC 13, HD 2*, #At 1, Dam 1d8+ poison, Mv 40', Sv F2, Ml 7, XP 100 ea.

HP	9 ☐☐☐☐☐ ☐☐☐☐
	8 ☐☐☐☐☐ ☐☐☐

Upper Level Key

1. PORTICO:

> Splintered stone steps rise to a landing lined by pillars containing carvings depicting some long-forgotten sea deity standing atop waves with people on bended knee making offerings. The pillars lead to a double stone door which stands slightly ajar.

If the party listens, growling and the sound of dogs eating will be heard beyond the door from area 2.

2. ENTRY CHAMBER:

> This once-beautiful entry chamber to the temple contains doors on both the east and west walls as well as a set of double doors north. The walls of this chamber have been desecrated and covered in graffiti. There are smears and pools of dried blood scattered throughout the entire chamber and the smell of rotting flesh assails your senses. A small pile of corpses, both human and humanoid has attracted the attention of a pack of emaciated dogs. They growl menacingly as they defend their gruesome meal.

The corpses are of goblins slain by Tarn's acolytes and of a member of Nebi's evil band who ran afoul of the giant hawks in area 14. The dogs are starving, desperate, and maddened from the influence of remaining evil of the temple and so will attack the party upon entry. If searched, there is nothing of value on the corpses other than a rusty goblin dagger or 2. The east and west doors are closed but have been recently forced and so will swing open with no resistance. The northern double doors however have been spiked shut by Nebi's men and will require either a turn spent to remove the spikes or combined Strength of >26 to force it open on a roll of 1-2 on 1d6. Keep in mind that the sounds at this door will alert the giant hawks in area 14.

If the players investigate the graffiti, they will find most of it in the goblin tongue proclaiming "V'rakknok wuz here" and "Gosh rulez" or similar (if the characters can read the goblin tongue). The only discernible lines written in common are "the undead hold the key" referring to area 16a and "beware door, it's a trap".

4 Dogs: AC 14, HD 1+1, #At 1+hold, Dam 1d4, Mv 50', Sv F1, Ml 9, XP 25 ea.

HP   6 ☐☐☐☐☐ ☐   5 ☐☐☐☐☐
     5 ☐☐☐☐☐   4 ☐☐☐☐

3. ACOLYTE'S CHAMBER:

> This room is dominated by a brick fireplace on the west wall. The furniture lies in splinters, scattered across the floor. Dusty cobwebs fill the corners near the ceiling and cast eerie shadows upon the walls from your light source. Something within the hearth glitters as it catches the light.

The glittering is from broken glass bottles and the cobwebs are harmless. There is nothing of interest in this room.

4. PRIEST'S CHAMBER:

> The west wall of this large chamber contains a brick fireplace and the north wall a door. A tattered carpet remains mostly intact upon the floor and a few pieces of decrepit furniture still stand along the eastern wall. You witness a horrifying sight: four dead humans lie in pools of fresh blood on the floor, some wearing the robes identifying them as members of your temple; they must be Tarn's men! A sole survivor wearing the now-bloody robes stands in the northwest corner of the room, holding his mace before a hulking figure clad in plate armor, shield, and bloody longsword. The massive man grins cruelly and rushes you with bloodlust in his eyes.

The large man is A'kk, the muscle of Nebi's band but certainly not the brains. The man in the robes is Nebi. The two had recently finished off Tarn and a few of his acolytes and Nebi is mockingly wearing Tarn's robes. Nebi thinks quickly on his feet and realizes his odds are better not attacking the party and so will assume the role of Tarn, even going so far as attacking A'kk with the party to gain their trust. Nebi will ride the party's confidence as long as possible in order to gain the treasure he believes is hidden in this temple but will try not to do any fighting unless necessary. He will slip away and escape or attempt to kill and rob the party, if the chance presents itself.

The furniture is mostly rotten and holds little of interest, some crumbling scrolls with accounting ledgers but there is a brick inside the chimney about 3' up which can be removed, behind which is secreted a rotting leather pouch containing 89 gp and 9 sp.

The corpses of Tarn and his men hold little other than chain armor, maces, and their holy symbols.

Nebi, Human Cleric 1: AC 18, #At 1, Dam 1d8, Mv 20', Ml 9, XP 25

CHA 14 (+1)

Equipment: plate mail, shield, mace, **Potion of Healing**, 16 gp

HP   5 ☐☐☐☐☐

A'kk, Human Fighter 1: AC 19, #At 1, Dam 1d8+1, Mv 20', Ml 9, XP 25

STR 15 (+1), DEX 13 (+1), CON 14 (+1)

Equipment: plate mail, shield, longsword, 35 gp

HP   8 ☐☐☐☐☐ ☐☐☐

5. SPIDER'S LAIR:

> The irregularly shaped room holds a brick fireplace on its northern wall, 2 once fine, but now rotting armchairs next to it, a bed on the west wall with a moldering dresser beside it. Debris is scattered along the floor of the room and something within the hearth glints in your light.

If inspected, the debris on the floor are scattered bones and bits of leather and mail, the indigestible bits left by this room's residents: 2 giant crab spiders. The glinting object in the hearth is one of the 3 **keys** needed on the lower level in order to obtain the second disk. The spiders slew and ate the key's owner long ago and it has remained as an invitation, luring the greedy into their trap. One spider makes its home up the chimney while the other lies in wait beneath the bed.

Trapped within the webbing inside the chimney, among a few skeletons, is some mundane armor and weapons as well as a beautiful dagger with a gem-encrusted scabbard worth 250 gp, and 2 small pouches containing 12 gp and 48 sp.

Within the webbing beneath the bed, besides a few mundane items, is a leather backpack containing 2 flasks of oil, 2 flasks of holy water, a 25' rope, and 1 **Potion of Cure Poison** with 2 doses.

2 Giant Crab Spiders: AC 13, HD 2*, #At 1,
Dam 1d8+ poison, Mv 40', Sv F2, Ml 7, XP 100 ea.

HP 12 □□□□□ □□□□□ □□
     7 □□□□□ □□

6. STAIRS LEADING TO MIDDLE LEVEL:

> Stone stairs spiral downward into the darkness here.

Note that when the party descends half of the stairs, the goblins watching the stairwell will shout an alarm "Bree-yark!" alerting area 16 while they retreat into area 15 and ready their defense.

7. GOBLINS' LAST STAND:

> This long chamber is bare save for the fur-clad goblins hiding within who now shriek a bloodthirsty battle cry and charge to attack with wicked blades drawn!

The door to this room has been spiked shut by the goblins cowering inside who fled attacks from both Tarn and Nebi's groups. Forcing the door requires rolling on 1d10 rather than 1d6, with the usual adjustments to the die roll range (i.e. 1-2 with a +1 bonus, 1-3 with a +2, and so on). Two characters can combine their efforts, adding their Strength bonuses together.

There are two goblins on the north and two on the south side of the door, so they will be able to attack from both sides.

4 Goblins: AC 14, HD 1-1, #At 1, Dam 1d6, Mv 20', Sv F1, Ml 7, XP 10 ea.

HP 4 □□□□   4 □□□□
     3 □□□   2 □□

Each has a tarnished short sword, furs acting as armor, and 8 sp.

8. INITIATE'S CHAMBERS:

> Rotting and moldering cots draped with thick cobwebs are the only things visible in this room.

This room is empty.

9. INITIATE'S CHAMBERS:

> Rotting and moldering cots are the only things, save for thick cobwebs, within this room. You think you hear water dripping somewhere nearby.

This room is empty.

10. INITIATE'S CHAMBERS:

> This room is empty except for a pile of smooth stones in the center of the room.

This room is empty.

11. INITIATES CHAMBERS:

> Rotten cots have been overturned and the remnants of a fire in the northeast corner are all you notice in this chamber.

This room is empty.

12. INITIATES CHAMBERS:

> Rotten cots have been smashed to bits and scattered about this room.

This room is empty.

13. HIGH STAKES POKER:

This irregularly shaped chamber houses 2 points of immediate interest. The first is a pile of corpses on the east wall, bearing the robes of your church. The second is the small table and chairs on the east wall where, until you entered, 4 armored men played cards. "Would you look at what we have here, Taravil? A couple of more contestants!" says a plate-clad dwarf now rising to his feet. "Ha ha, yeah! A couple more is what we gots! I'm gonna' bash em' real good!" chimes in his tall plate-clad companion. The other 2 men at the table wear leather, they grasp their blades and stand smirking at you.

The door to this chamber has been forced and so opens easily. These 4 men are from Nebi's party and will be playing cards at the table unless the party is making a lot of noise before entering in which case, they will be ready to attack. If Nebi is with the player's group, he may see his opportunity to surprise the players by turning on them. The corpses in the corner were members of Tarn's acolytes who met an untimely end at the hands of these villains. The corpses wear leather beneath their robes and have only maces and holy symbols. The card table has a deck of playing cards, 94 gp, 144 sp, 75 cp, and a dented silver goblet worth 25 gp. Silbach wears a gold ring with a gem worth 180 gp, and there is a pack containing 4 weeks preserved rations and as much water along with 50' rope, 12 iron spikes w/ hammer, chalk, whetstone, armor polishing kit, and 2 steel mirrors.

Silbach, Dwarf Fighter 1: AC 17, #At 1, Dam 1d10, Mv 20', MI 9, XP 25

INT 17 (+2), WIS 14 (+1), DEX 8 (-1)

Equipment: plate mail, great axe

HP   6   ☐☐☐☐☐ ☐

Taravil, Human Fighter 1: AC 18, #At 1, Dam 1d8, Mv 20', MI 9, XP 25

INT 5 (-2), CON 16 (+2)

Equipment: plate mail, shield, battle axe

HP   5   ☐☐☐☐☐

Slink, Human Thief 1: AC 14, #At 1, Dam 1d8, Mv 30', MI 9, XP 25

STR 14 (+1), INT 7 (-1), DEX 15 (+1), CHA 8 (-1)

Equipment: leather armor, scimitar

HP   2   ☐☐

Slimp, Human Thief 1: AC 14, #At 1, Dam 1d8, Mv 40', MI 9, XP 25

CON 13 (+1)

Equipment: **Leather Armor +1**, longsword

HP   3   ☐☐☐

14. GIANT HAWK'S LAIR:

This room was clearly once a grand center of worship of the sea god. Crumbling columns flank the sides of the chamber as does debris and splintered furniture. The northeastern wall and much of the ceiling to this room has crumbled and stands open to the elements. You can't help but marvel at the breathtaking view of the sea from this vantage point. A raised area holding the old altar stands to the north and atop it rests a massive nest made of sticks, branches, and pieces of old pews. You stand in a puddle of blood and the eviscerated remains of a man that has been torn to shreds lies roughly 10 feet ahead of you. Loud squawking echoes from the walls and is almost too loud to stand.

This area is now the lair of a mated pair of giant hawks and their young. They have made a nest atop the altar and use the open walls and ceilings to fly in and out to hunt the countryside. Nebi and his men stumbled into this area and succeeded in putting an arrow into one of the hawks before being driven out, suffering 2 casualties in the process. If the party took more than 1 round to open the door, the alerted hawks will swoop to attack, surprising 1-4 on a 1d6.

The corpse of Nebi's man wears shredded chainmail, a shield, short sword, short bow with 18 arrows, 2 torches, 1 week's preserved rations, and 28 gp.

The hawks nest contains a hatchling who does not fight as it is too young. Mixed amongst the nest is: 167 gp, 2 small gems worth 50 gp each, 1 **Scroll of Cure Light Wounds** (2 uses), and 1 gold necklace with an ornate pendant worth 500 gp that belonged to the Slateholm jeweler's daughter who was out riding her horse when she became a meal. If the party tries to sell the pendant in Slateholm the jeweler will assume the party murdered and robbed his daughter and will either involve the town watch or hire assassins; it is up to

the GM. If the altar is cleared off and searched, it contains a secret compartment containing 230 gp and 15 small gems worth 20 gp each.

2 Giant Hawks: AC 14, HD 4, #At 1, Dam 1d6, Mv 150' (10'), Sv F4, Ml 12 (due to young), XP 240 ea.

HP 26 ☐☐☐☐☐ ☐☐☐☐☐ ☐☐☐☐☐ ☐☐☐☐☐
         ☐☐☐☐☐ ☐

     21 ☐☐☐☐☐ ☐☐☐☐☐ ☐☐☐☐☐ ☐☐☐☐☐
         ☐

Middle Level Key

15. GUARDIANS OF THE STAIRWELL:

> There are goblins in this room, goblins who knew you were coming and launch a volley of sling stones from behind an overturned table to greet you.

The door to this room has been previously kicked in so is not locked and swings open easily. There are 4 goblins here tasked with watching the stairs and shouting an alarm to warn area 16. They have overturned a heavy oaken table and are using it for cover as they fire sling stones at the party. If the party returns fire, they will suffer a -3 to hit penalty as the goblins are using the table as cover. When the party closes, the goblins draw short swords for melee. Note that after 4 rounds, the occupants of area 16 will have ascended the stairs and will flank the party.

Each goblin has a sling with stones, short sword, and 6 sp. There is an unlocked wooden chest in the room containing 47 gp, 186 sp, and a silver brooch worth 80 gp.

4 Goblins: AC 14, HD 1-1, #At 1, Dam 1d3 or 1d6, Mv 20', Sv F1, Ml 7, XP 10 ea.

HP   5 ☐☐☐☐☐   4 ☐☐☐☐
     4 ☐☐☐☐   3 ☐☐☐

16. GOBLIN LEADER'S QUARTERS:

> This room contains a moldering bed and dresser as well as piles of furs along the floors. The room smells of urine and body odor. There is a door on the west wall.

A goblin warrior and his concubines reside here and will race from bed to join the fray in area 15 once the alarm is given.

The dresser contains a **Scroll of Bless**, 135 gp, and a book of goblin love poems worth 50 gp to the right buyer.

The door leading to area 16a is locked.

Goblin Warrior: AC 14, HD 3-3, #At 1, Dam 1d6, Mv 20', Sv F1, Ml 8, XP 145

HP 17   ☐☐☐☐☐ ☐☐☐☐☐ ☐☐☐☐☐ ☐☐

2 Unarmored Concubines: AC 14, HD 1-1, #At 1, Dam 1d4, Mv 30', Sv F1, Ml 8, XP 10 ea.

HP 2 ☐☐   2 ☐☐

16A. TRAPPED KEY ROOM:

The door leading to this area is locked. This 10'x10' room looks just like an empty closet but the floor of the room is an illusion and masks a 10'x10' pit causing 1d6 points of damage, with a successful save vs. Death Ray resulting in half damage. The illusion is designed so that anyone witnessing a character fall will see them simply disappear soundlessly. Within the pit permanent **darkness** and **silence** have been cast, so once inside the character is blind (-4 to hit; see the Core Rules for details) and deaf/mute (cannot cast spells nor call

for help). To make matters worse, there are 2 undead skeletons lurking within the trapped pit, waiting to lash out upon the living. These skeletons cannot see the PCs any more than the PCs can see them, but in such a small space they will surely bump into each other. The GM should run this fight however he or she sees fit.

One of the three **keys** needed to unlock the disk on the lower level is also in the pit. Each round that a character moves, he or she has a 1-2 on 1d6 chance of accidentally kicking or stepping on it.

The secret door noted on the map is in the back wall of the pit, and can be found on normal odds by feeling around the wall with a normal chance of success (as it is hidden mostly by the darkness).

2 Skeletons: AC 13, HD 1, #At 1, Dam 1d6, Mv 40', Sv F1, Ml 12, XP 25 ea.

HP 5 ☐☐☐☐☐   4 ☐☐☐☐

17. ENCHANTED PORTCULLIS WITH A DISK:

> You stand at a portcullis which seems to hum with energy. Beyond you see a room humbly furnished but seemingly untouched by time. There is a small wooden pedestal against the western wall with a golden disk atop, about 12" in diameter and bearing a holy symbol. The only other feature of interest in this room is a lever directly across from where you stand on the western wall; the lever is in the upward position.

The only entrance into this room is the trap door in the ceiling, accessed from area 18. The portcullis is enchanted and will resist all attempts to open it. If the party somehow devises a clever way to throw the switch on the opposite wall, this triggers a trap. The lever is actually a spring-loaded spear and will launch itself at the portcullis, striking as a 3 HD monster and causing 1d6 points of damage unless a save vs. Death Ray is made; a successful save means the spear hit the portcullis instead of the intended victim.

The pedestal is unremarkable, and the **golden disk** is one of a pair needed to open the sealed door leading to area 33.

18. CHAMBER OF JUDGMENT:

This chamber is completely empty and your light casts eerie shadows upon the walls, shadows begin to dance and then pull themselves off of the wall and form a spectral being which points toward you menacingly. You feel your blood run ice cold and your hair stands up on its end.

If Nebi still remains in the group, then the party is judged unworthy, read the following:

The spirit opens its mouth impossibly wide and the words explode into your minds, "Unworthy! One of you is Unworthy! Do not return until you are clean." You suddenly find yourselves back in the hallway, in front of the closed door leading to the room where you met the apparition.

If Nebi (or anyone else blatantly evil) is no longer in the group, then read the following:

The spirit opens its mouth impossibly wide and the words explode into your minds, "Worthy! You have been deemed worthy!" The spirit fades and a door appears in the eastern wall.

The secret room connected to this area is a short corridor leading to an open 5' square pit. A set of iron rungs leads down 50' into the darkness, opening into a 10' cubical room with a trap door in the floor. It is this trap door that connects to room 17, above (which, perhaps somewhat confusingly, is below room 18).

19. SECRET STOREROOM:

This small closet seems to have been forgotten for centuries. A small shelf contains stoppered bottles, a few rolled pieces of parchment, and an amulet on an iron chain.

The secret door is opened by depressing a stone on the wall. This was used as a storage area by the original high priests of the sea god. There are 2 **Potions of Healing**, 1 **Potion of Haste**, 1 **Scroll of Protection from Evil and Cure Light Wounds**, 1 **Scroll of Bless**, and 1 **Amulet of Protection from Undead** (grants the wearer +1 AC vs. undead).

20. BASIN OF BLESSINGS:

This room has a door on both the north and south walls. The floor to the west has a small stone pedestal with stone basin containing brackish water. There is a silver goblet resting on the basin.

This was part of the original temple and a ritual area. Now the water here is stagnant and diseased and if consumed the character must save vs. Poison or become violently ill for 1d8 hours, fighting at -2 both to hit and damage, and must save vs. Poison every hour affected or spend one turn vomiting loudly, attracting wandering monsters on 1-3 on 1d6. The goblet is worth 50 gp.

21. ARMORED GUARDIANS:

This large room is empty save for the door on the northern wall and 2 suits of full plate armor standing on each side, bearing crossed halberds.

If the party does not have Nebi in it (or anyone else blatantly evil), once approached the armor will animate and uncross the halberds, allowing the party to pass. If, however Nebi (or anyone else blatantly evil) is in the party, the armor will animate and attack. The armor is not undead so cannot be turned but is mindless and so is unaffected by magic requiring a living brain such as **charm** or **sleep**. The armor and halberds will crumble to rusted bits once defeated.

2 Animated Armors: AC 18, HD 1, #At 1, Dam 1d10, Mv 20', Sv F1, Ml 12, XP 25 ea.

HP   5 ☐☐☐☐☐   4 ☐☐☐☐

Lower Level Key

22. HOBGOBLIN LEADER:

This room is bare other than doors along the southern and western walls. 3 goblins stand around a red-orange skinned brute wielding a long sword and barking out what you can only surmise are orders.

Unless the party is loudly approaching, the hobgoblin and goblins will be surprised on a roll of 1-3 on 1d6 as the leader is trying to regain control of his terrified troops after their assault north and encounters with traps and undead. The hobgoblin is the leader of the goblins in the temple and is unaware of the fate of his troops on the upper levels. He is not stupid and will seek to flee or strike a bargain if battle goes poorly. He wears a silver chain worth 35 gp and has a pouch containing 41 gp and 80 sp. The goblins each have 12 sp.

Hobgoblin: AC 14, HD 1, #At 1, Dam 1d8, Mv 30', Sv F1, Ml 8, XP 25

HP   7   ☐☐☐☐☐ ☐☐

3 Goblins: AC 14, HD 1-1, #At 1, Dam 1d6, Mv 20', Sv F1, Ml 7 XP 10 ea.

HP   4 ☐☐☐☐   4   ☐☐☐☐
       2 ☐☐

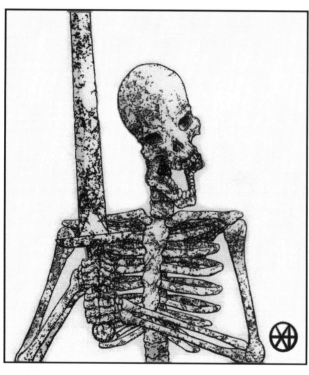

23. SKELETAL STORAGE:

> Bones of the animated dead wield deadly, rusted blades which they are using to carve the flesh from writhing and contorting fallen goblins. In unison, they stop their gruesome act and train their hollow eye sockets upon you then lurch forward, swinging their lethal swords in wide arcs as they approach.

The goblins broke through the door here only to find that a group of skeletons lay in wait. The undead butchered 3 goblins as the others fled. Their corpses have 8 sp each, a tarnished short sword, and wooden buckler.

5 Skeletons: AC 13, HD 1, #At 1, Dam 1d6, Mv 40', Sv F1, Ml 12, XP 25 ea.

HP   5 ☐☐☐☐☐   5   ☐☐☐☐☐
       5 ☐☐☐☐☐   4   ☐☐☐☐
       3 ☐☐☐

24. UNLUCKY GOBLIN AND SKELETAL STORAGE:

> The door to this chamber is ajar with the corpse of a goblin lying in the threshold, preventing it from closing. The goblin has a spear impaling its chest and lies in a pool of blood.

The goblin sprung a spear trap when opening the door. Within the small room wait 2 skeletons that will attack anyone entering. The goblin has 12 sp in addition to his sword and shield.

2 Skeletons: AC 13, HD 1, #At 1, Dam 1d6, Mv 40', Sv F1, Ml 12, XP 25 ea.

HP   5 ☐☐☐☐☐   5   ☐☐☐☐☐

25. KEYHOLE ROOM:

> Other than multiple sets of footprints through the dust of this room, it appears to be quite empty. You think you hear footsteps in the hallway to the north, but you cannot be sure.

The room is empty, and the footsteps are a trick of the imagination. The only thing of interest in this room is the secret door which, if searched for, the players will find a keyhole in the stone wall. Any one of the three **keys** may be inserted and turned and there will be a loud click, the key cannot be removed. Nothing more will happen until the third key is inserted and turned (area 25, 26, and 32 contain key holes) at which point all three secret doors will grind open, revealing area 27.

26. KEYHOLE ROOM:

> This room is bare other than dust along the floor and cobwebs in southwest corner of the ceiling. A rusted and dented helmet lies in the southwest corner and the stub of a burned torch rests at your feet upon the floor at the door.

The only thing of interest in this room is the secret door which, if searched for, the players will find a keyhole in the stone wall. Any one of the three **keys** may be inserted and turned and there will be a loud click, the key cannot be removed. Nothing more will happen until the third key is inserted and turned (area 25, 26, and 32 contain key holes) at which point all three secret doors will grind open, revealing area 27.

27. GOLDEN DISK AND ITS GUARDIAN:

> The third key turns and its click echoes throughout the silent temple; a cool breeze briefly blows from somewhere then abruptly stops. A deafening grinding sound accompanies the wall before you slowly swinging open to reveal a hidden chamber beyond.

This is the chamber holding one of the 2 golden disks which will open the sealed doors at area 28. As the party approaches the alcove in the middle of the chamber where the number 27 is on the map, read or paraphrase the following:

> A wooden statue of a beautiful woman is standing in this alcove; she wears the carved robes of a priestess. In her outstretched arms she presents a golden disk, about 12 inches in diameter bearing the engraving of a holy symbol.

The party may take the disk without issue so long as Nebi (or any other blatantly evil character) is not with them. If the party has an evil character, the statue will animate and defend the disk. Note that a wood golem may not be harmed by non-magical weapons, but fire causes +1 point per die of damage. Wood golems also suffer a -1 initiative penalty.

Wood Golem: AC 13, HD 2+2, #At 1, Dam 1d8, Mv 40', Sv F1, Ml 12, XP 100

HP 12   ☐☐☐☐☐ ☐☐☐☐☐ ☐☐

28. THE SEALED DOOR:

> Massive stone double doors stand here, each having a circular impression about 12" in diameter carved out at about chest height. Ornately engraved across the doors is the following verse:
>
> *One disk of gold when laid in its hole,*
>
> > *opens the path to its twin.*
>
> *Thrice turn the keys, prepared must ye be,*
>
> > *to conquer the horror within.*

The doorway is magically sealed and will resist all efforts to open it. Both **golden disks** (found at areas 17 and 27) must be inserted in order to break the magical seal and open the doorway. Once both disks are inserted, there will be a flash and the doors will swing open inwardly.

29. ALCHEMY LAB:

> This room contains still sturdy wooden tables and chairs as well as an assortment of broken glass strewn across the tables and floor. There is an acrid smell to the air here.

This room housed a small alchemy lab for the temple, but the goblins and hobgoblin found it first and smashed everything to bits. There is nothing salvageable in this room.

30. KEY CHAMBER:

> This room curiously contains only a small table in its center, a chest roughly 1'x1' rests atop the table.

The box is unlocked and contains one of the three **keys** needed to open the way to area 27. The box is however trapped with poison gas that will fill the room if not properly detected (+20%) and removed (+15%) first. The gas has weakened over the years and lost its killer quality and allows a save vs. Poison at +2 as well as causing only choking for 1d4 turns, resulting in -2 to hit and damage rolls.

31. CLERIC SUPPLY CLOSET:

> Shelves filled with moldering books and boxes as well as a few stoppered vials rest here, long forgotten until now.

The books are various ledgers but two are old holy books containing the history of the sea god's worshipers and would be worth 100 gp as a set to the right buyer. The boxes contain prayer beads and incense and would be worth 35 gp for the lot. There are four vials of holy water on the shelves.

32. KEYHOLE ROOM:

> Water drips from a crack in the ceiling in of the southwest corner of this room, forming a small pool. This room seems otherwise empty.

The only thing of interest in this room is the secret door which, if searched for, the players will find a keyhole in the stone wall. Any one of the three **keys** may be inserted and turned and there will be a loud click, the key cannot be removed. Nothing more will happen until the third key is inserted and turned (area 25, 26, and 32 contain key holes) at which point all three secret doors will grind open, revealing area 27.

33. THE HORROR WITHIN:

> You descend the stone steps which end on a raised area flanked by pillars with engravings depicting the sea god atop waves. The foul odor of decay assails your senses as you make your way into the dimly illuminated interior. With each step, you feel a chill setting in and can feel the tangible evil of this room. This was clearly one the temple's main chambers, where the high priests came to make offerings and worship. Now your light casts away the inky blackness for the first time in a century. As you step onto the landing at the end of the stairs, hundreds of crimson and ebony candles lining the entire chamber flicker into flaming life, illuminating this inner temple. From behind the northernmost pillars on both the left and right, step figures shrouded in dark robes with cowls obscuring their faces but still you see a red glow where their eyes should be. The figures seem almost to float as they make their way toward you. A guttural snarl sends a shiver through you as just beyond the robed figures you behold a truly fearsome sight: lumbering toward you from an altar at the northernmost part of the temple, its festering corpse riddled with wriggling vermin, is a massive putrid and rotting hobgoblin, a crown of iron attached to its skull with rusted spikes. The colossal nauseating abomination drags with it an enormous and wicked looking great axe.

The two robed figures are the undead embodiment of two evil high priests imprisoned here, they raised the hobgoblin chief as an undead zombie beast. The sealed door contained these evil beings, now they must be dealt with or they will escape the temple, raising any dead the beings come across, and ravage the land with an ever-growing army. The undead hobgoblin chief wields the magical great axe +1 it used in life. This room is an unholy place and so Clerics cannot turn the undead. The 2 robed figures are **crimson bones skeletons** and fall to a pile of bones when reduced to 0 HP, only to rise again in 1d4 rounds with half their previous HP and continue to do so until targeted by a **bless** spell or doused with holy water. The hobgoblin is huge but, in all respects, simply a 3 HD zombie wielding a **Great Axe +1**.

2 Crimson Bones Skeletons: AC 13, HD 2, #At 1, Dam 1d6, Mv 50', Sv F2, Ml 12, XP 100 ea.

HP 12 ☐☐☐☐☐ ☐☐☐☐☐ ☐☐
     11 ☐☐☐☐☐ ☐☐☐☐☐ ☐

Hulking Hobgoblin Chief Zombie: AC 12, HD 3, #At 1, Dam 1d10+1, Mv 20', Sv F3, Ml 12, XP 175

HP 19 ☐☐☐☐☐ ☐☐☐☐☐ ☐☐☐☐☐ ☐☐☐☐

With the destruction of the undead, the evil is lifted from this place. The altar is smeared with all forms of unholy desecration but if searched, contains a secret compartment containing 276 gp, a beautiful ceremonial dagger worth 175 gp, **2 Potions of Healing**, and 12 small gems worth 30 gp each.

With the temple cleared, the party may triumphantly return to Slateholm with the news of their glorious victory over evil, but also with the sad news of Tarn's ill-fated expedition. The priest will reward the party by healing them all of their wounds as well as granting one Cleric a holy weapon: a **Cudgel +1** (1d4+1) which acts as a holy symbol and has a 10% chance every time a successful hit is scored against an undead opponent of flashing a holy light which damages all undead in a 10' radius, causing 1d4 points of damage to each.

Concluding the Adventure

With the successful clearing of the temple, each character will be rewarded 500 XP in addition to XP earned during the adventure and whatever XP bonus for good role play you see fit. The party will surely be local heroes with tales forever told of these brave souls vanquishing The Horror Within.

Three Days Of Peace And Music
by Sean Wellington

Introduction

A huge festival drawing thousands of visitors to the site of an ancient temple is underway.

Legend has it that a doomsday cult built the structure centuries ago, and abandoned it after the world failed to end as predicted by their charismatic leader. The area has since been reclaimed by farm, field and forest many times over, and today the temple is a picturesque ruin surrounded by grasslands and gently rolling hills. Most recently, ownership of the property has passed into the hands of a local dairy farmer who uses the land to pasture his herds. The crumbling temple now serves variously as a barn, shed and storehouse.

Earlier this year, promoters pitching the "largest music and art fair the realm has ever seen" approached the farmer seeking to use his land as a venue. For reasons known only to himself, he agreed to their plan and preparations soon began. Excitement has been building for months, and thousands of creatives, curiosity seekers, revelers, music lovers and plain-old weirdos have flocked to the site. The bucolic area is now abuzz with activity on a scale never seen before.

The upper level of the temple has been converted by the festival organizers into a makeshift headquarters, while the lower levels have been cordoned off by security in the interest of safety. Perhaps unsurprisingly for an event of this size, unexpected contingencies have arisen. The weather has soured, and days of chilly rain have turned the surrounding fields into a sea of mud. The large crowd seems to be taking everything in stride (for now), but the organizers worry that the situation could quickly devolve into total chaos should spirits fall. Disturbingly, one of the headlining performers has suddenly vanished and a weird shimmering apparition has appeared in the apse of the ruined temple. Tension among the staff is high enough already and these last-minute developments have done little to help the situation.

It is sundown on the eve of the festival's opening day. The PCs have been approached by management to help locate the missing performer, who was last seen entering the basement of the temple, despite it clearly being posted off limits. No one yet knows of his disappearance besides the Festival Director and Chief of Security who are hoping to resolve the situation quickly... and discreetly.

The show must go on!

GM Background

While the history of the temple and its builder, Timoteo, is obscure to the point of being forgotten, the events that happened here centuries ago will prove to have a very palpable impact on the present day. To say that the site and timing of the festival are inauspicious is an understatement of the highest magnitude.

But first some background: all Eschatonomancers know that calling the end of the world is tricky business. Few will admit (openly, at any rate) that it's really just a numbers game. A matter of probabilities rather than certainties; of having the right magic in the right place at the right time. As such, it is common practice for would-be Immanetizers to seek every possible advantage to improve their odds, including bringing in outside help. And Timoteo was no exception.

Having located a site at the rare intersection of four ley lines, Timoteo and his followers built a base for their nefarious operations. On the eve of an ominous, million-year syzygy, they would open a gate allowing certain malevolent extraplanar entities to enter our universe at the temple. The combination of the location, planetary alignment and Timoteo's proprietary magic would energize these beings beyond all imagination, and the havoc they would wreak would certainly bring about the destruction of life as we know it. Or so the plan went.

So confident in his calculations was Timoteo that he ordered his followers to sacrifice him on the temple's altar as the gate was being opened, in order that his rotten soul might have an unobstructed view of the destruction that was to unfold. Alas, when they performed that dark ritual, nothing happened and the moment passed.

Thinking they must have made some procedural error, his followers attempted to repeat the procedure over the next few nights. New victims were chosen from the group's ranks each time, and equally disappointing results were obtained. Discouraged by their lack of success and dwindling numbers, the remaining cultists mummified Timoteo and interred him along with the corpses of the other sacrifices in the lowest levels of the temple. Without his strong leadership, the doomsday project faltered and the group disbanded soon thereafter.

In retrospect, Timoteo's process would have been devastatingly effective had it not suffered from an off-by-one error in the formula for calculating the current millennium. Unbeknownst to the cultists, a gate was indeed created that night, but one that would not open for another thousand years. And as luck would have it, the millennial anniversary of that ritual coincides precisely with the eve of the festival.

Absent the rare astronomical conjunction and support of Timoteo's (thankfully lost) incantations, the opening of the gate in the present day is somewhat less dire than originally intended. In fact, were the temple not thronged with the vital energy of thousands of hyped-up concert goers, the whole thing might even have gone unnoticed, with the portal languishing as yet another cosmic by-way through the backwaters of the multiverse.

Unfortunately, this is not to be the case. The madcap energy of the nearby festival has attracted the interest of a being known as **Vheld'broggn**, an eldritch horror from the Deep Beyond that sees the present scene, if not the entire world around it, as a rich banquet for its abominable appetites.

All portals tend to lose their shape over time, and after a thousand years without maintenance, Timoteo's gate is today more akin to a tunnel. It will therefore take Vheld'broggn several days to fully cross over from its vile dimension into our own, a process that is already underway and will complete at sundown on the festival's final day.

Time is of the essence: the PCs must find a way to close the gate or they will have to deal with Vheld'broggn.

Schedule of Events

Of course, before they can close the gate, the PCs must learn of its existence and come to understand the ramifications of Vheld'broggn's arrival.

The scenario begins with the PCs being summoned to meet the festival's Director, Charmise. She will relate the disappearance of the show's headliner, Jay Sylvanpool, and solicit their assistance in locating him, offering to pay whatever it takes, out of her own pocket if necessary, to secure the party's assistance. Sylvanpool was last seen descending into the lower levels of the temple at area 6 earlier today. Charmise will mention the appearance of the hourglass in area 14, almost as an afterthought, but she is entirely focused on the festival and her priority is locating the missing performer.

The apparition should be a strong indicator to the PCs that something odd is happening, and once the gate is discovered in area 33, there should be no doubt that trouble is coming but fast.

With each passing hour, Vheld'broggn's journey brings it closer to our dimension. As it approaches, its presence is collapsing the minds of those of lesser will (particularly the crowd), who are becoming increasingly more agitated and hostile as time passes. The GM should initially reflect this as an increasing sense of worry and anxiety amongst the festival staff and guards.

As the sun rises on the festival's opening day, it reveals that a thick fog has descended, reducing visibility to 5' outside the temple exterior. This fog will not lift as the day progresses and will remain in effect throughout the adventure.

Throughout the following days, there will be random fights and outbursts of violence in the crowd, which will cause the guards to be periodically called away from the temple. By noon of the second day, these will have escalated into a full-blown riot, and the temple will be surrounded by raving concert-goers. At this point, the guards will seal the doors and the PCs may no longer leave the temple proper. The rioters, inflamed by Vheld'broggn's madness, will be drawn to the temple and will attempt to break in and enter its lower levels.

In the middle of the night prior to the final day, Charmise will somehow manage to escape, taking all of the festival's cash with her. One of the female guards will be discovered missing soon thereafter.

At sundown of the final day, Vheld'broggn will emerge fully in area 33. It will make his way directly to the surface, attacking anyone it encounters on the way. Once it has exited the temple, it will proceed to massacre the crowd in the most gruesome manner possible, slaying any and all that cross its path.

Because of this schedule, it is vitally important that the GM keep accurate track of time. Many of the events and encounters in the dungeon are designed to waste time, thus increasing the likelihood of Vheld'broggn crossing into our dimension. The GM may accelerate the pace of these events if the party is making faster progress through the temple than anticipated.

Due to Vheld'broggns presence, any food and water brought by the PCs into the lower levels of the temple will spoil within 1 hour. The party must return to the upper level to eat and fully rest.

Pictures at an (Eldritch) Exposition

Among the other effects of Vheld'broggn's approach are the sudden appearance of unnatural creatures and weird apparitions throughout the temple, such as the ghostly hourglass in area 14. Some of these illusions reveal scenes from the temple's history and are intended to provide the party with clues regarding the forces currently at work. When such an illusion manifests, it will present as a three-dimensional, semi-transparent scene, repeating in a loop in the spot where it was encountered. Watching each scene completely will take 3 full turns of game time, as will each repeat visit should the PCs wish to see a replay.

The man depicted in the scenes is the temple's long-forgotten architect, Timoteo. The PCs will not be able to identify him as such, but will recognize him as the same person from scene to scene, although time will have passed and he may appear older or younger.

Likewise, various objects presented in the scenes can also be found in the dungeon:

- Ruby Pendant (area 32)
- Curved Dagger (area 20)
- Small Octagonal Frame (area 23)
- Golden Brazier (area 23)

Each of these objects is immediately recognizable if the PCs have previously seen it in one of the illusions. The GM should seed the notion that the gate was opened by magic involving these objects and, by implication, can be closed by using them together in some way as well. However, there is no set recipe for doing so – the GM should present the visions, insinuate and hint, and let the PCs' imagination take it from there. Any reasonable attempt to use them together to close the gate in area 33 should be rewarded with success.

If the PCs do not discover the illusions on their own, the GM should feel free to improvise ways of making their content known to the party (e.g. appearing in dreams, or as the result of spell misfires, etc.).

WEIRD SCENE #1:

A young, dark haired man dressed in the robes of the Necromancers' Guild intently scribbles on a blackboard, which is covered with strange symbols and lengthy calculations. A bowl of burning charcoal sits atop an ornately decorated golden tripod on a desk behind him. The man periodically consults the fire as he proceeds with his writing, as if seeing something in its glowing embers.

This is a scene from Timoteo's days as a graduate student when he was conducting the breakthrough research behind his magic. A magic user or elf that studies the writings will recognize them as a highly unorthodox form of portal magic, although the specific details will elude their comprehension. Additionally, they may recognize the techniques and formulae being used as belonging to darkest schools of magic, ones that are rightfully forbidden in civilized realms.

WEIRD SCENE #2

A figure in purple robes struggles as others in similar dress drag him to a bloody stone table. The captive wears a pendant with a large red stone around his neck. As they hold him down, another figure emerges holding a sinister curved dagger, which he plunges repeatedly into the neck and chest of the restrained man. The robed figures watch as their victim dies, but seem dismayed by their efforts.

This scene depicts the cultists' failed attempts to perform Timoteo's ritual. The dagger and pendant are the same as the ones used in the other scenes, but the pendant is no longer glowing. As the scene repeats, it will show different victims meeting a similarly gory demise.

WEIRD SCENE #3

Various hooded figures stand on the porch of a magnificent building receiving gifts of coin, livestock and other finery from a long line of supplicants as if in tribute. A black-haired man wearing a pendant with a glowing red stone, stands off to the side, presiding over the scene. Those presenting the gifts appear nervous and frightened, the gifts are carried into the temple through a large double door.

The is a scene of the temple in its heyday, with the cultists receiving levies imposed on their subject population. The PCs may recognize this as the front porch of the building.

WEIRD SCENE #4

A man with long black hair sits at a desk piled high with tomes and scrolls. A small golden tripod holding a burning brazier stands on the desk amidst the clutter. The flames dance and take on the shape of strange creatures that jump into his hand through a small octagonal metal frame that he holds, fizzling out as he catches them.

This is a scene from Timoteo's study in which he develops the magic for opening the gate. The octagonal frame and brazier can be found in area 23.

WEIRD SCENE #5

A man with long black hair directs a group of workers who are mounting a large octagonal frame to the wall of an underground chamber. The frame is made of a strange black material that seems to absorb, rather than reflect the light of their torches.

Here Timoteo's followers are preparing the gate in the temple's Great Hall. Any PC that has seen area 33 or the image of Timoteo at his tripod will recognize the connection immediately. The tripod itself can be found in area 23.

WEIRD SCENE #6

A naked man, with long graying black hair and a Fu Manchu mustache, leans against an upright stone table with arms crossed. He is surrounded by several hooded figures in dark purple robes. Around his neck hangs a pendant with a large red stone, which glows slightly. Another figure appears suddenly brandishing a wicked looking curved dagger, which he plunges into the chest of the man, who remains serenely calm during the procedure. The glow of the pendant fades as he dies.

This scene depicts the sacrifice of Timoteo. The pendant can be found around the neck of his mummy in area 32 and the dagger is in area 20.

Wandering Monsters

Check for random encounters by rolling 1d6 every three hours, as follows:

1. On day 1: a roll of 1 indicates an encounter;

2. On day 2: a roll of 1 or 2 indicates an encounter;

3. On day 3: a roll of 1, 2 or 3 indicates an encounter.

Roll 2d8 to select the encounter, or choose from the list below. If a Weird Scene is indicated that has already been presented to the PCs, select a different one or treat as an encounter with 1d8 rioters per encounter 16 below.

2. **1d10 Stirges:**
AC 13, HD 1*, #At 1 bite, Dam 1d4+1d4/round blood drain, Mv 10' Fly 60', Sv F1, MI 9, XP 37 ea.

HP	6 □□□□□ □	5 □□□□□
	3 □□□	4 □□□□
	5 □□□□□	5 □□□□□
	6 □□□□□ □	6 □□□□□ □
	5 □□□□□	4 □□□□

3. **Weird Scene #1**

4. **2d6 Flashbags:**
See "New Monsters" below.
AC 10, HD 1 hp, #At 1 explosion, Dam blindness, Mv 20', Sv NM, MI 12, XP 25 ea.
Each checkbox represents one monster.

HP   12   □□□□□ □□□□□ □□

5. **Weird Scene #2**

6. **1d3 Tentacle Worms (3 total):**
AC 13, HD 3*, #At 6 tentacles, Dam paralysis, Mv 40', Sv F3, MI 9, XP 175 ea.

HP	12 □□□□□ □□□□□ □□
	18 □□□□□ □□□□□ □□□□□ □□□
	16 □□□□□ □□□□□ □□□□□ □

7. **Weird Scene #3**

8. **Boggart:**
From the **Basic Fantasy Field Guide Volume 1.**
AC 14, HD 6*, #At 2 claws, Dam 1d6 claw, Mv 40', Sv MU1, MI 7, XP 555

HP   12   □□□□□ □□□□□ □□

9. **Weird Scene #4**

10. **1d3 Feral Dogs:**
AC 14, HD 1+1, #At 1 bite, Dam 1d4+1 + hold, Mv 50', Sv F1, MI 9, XP 25 ea.

HP	6 □□□□□ □	5 □□□□□
	7 □□□□□ □□	4 □□□□
	8 □□□□□ □□□	4 □□□□
	6 □□□□□ □	5 □□□□□
	5 □□□□□	6 □□□□□ □
	5 □□□□□	4 □□□□

11. **Weird Scene #5**

12. **1d4 Awful Offal:**
See "New Monsters" below.
AC 13, HD 2, #At 1 bile spit/secretion, Dam 1d8, Mv 20', Sv F2, MI 12, XP 75 ea.

HP	5 □□□□□
	8 □□□□□ □□□
	8 □□□□□ □□□
	11 □□□□□ □□□□□ □

13. **Weird Scene #6**

14. **Quasit:**
From the **Basic Fantasy Field Guide Volume 1.**
AC 19‡, HD 2**, #At 2 claws/1 bite, Dam 1d2+poison/1d3 bite, Mv 30', Sv MU2, MI 7, XP 125

HP   10   □□□□□ □□□□□

15. **1d4 Grimlock:**
From the **Basic Fantasy Field Guide Volume 1.**
AC 15, HD 2, #At 1 battleaxe, Dam 1d8, Mv 30', Sv F2, MI 7, XP 75 ea.

HP	10 □□□□□ □□□□□
	10 □□□□□ □□□□□
	10 □□□□□ □□□□□
	10 □□□□□ □□□□□

16. **1d8 Rioters:**
Festival attendees that have succumbed to Vheld'brognn's chaotic madness and broken into the temple. They attack with their fists or improvised weapons, such as rocks or sticks and will try to set fires with their torches. Treat as no encounter if the riot has not yet occurred.
AC 11, HD 5 HP, #At 1 fists, improvised weapon or torches, Dam 1d4+1, Mv 50', Sv NM, MI 7, XP 25 ea.

HP	5 □□□□□	5 □□□□□
	5 □□□□□	5 □□□□□
	5 □□□□□	5 □□□□□
	5 □□□□□	5 □□□□□

Festival Environment

The festival is situated in a remote area that is two days' travel by foot from the nearest small village and a full week's journey from any major city. Town amenities and supplies are generally unavailable. However, the event has attracted a number of vendors and a marketplace of sorts has sprung up. Until the riot breaks out and the temple is closed off, the PCs may venture out into the crowd and find the following goods and services for sale:

1. Food
2. Fuel/Oil/Wood/Tinder
3. Trinkets/Gadgets
4. Fortune telling and divination
5. Minor healing
6. Any and all manner of intoxicants

All prices are marked up 25% above what is listed in the **Basic Fantasy Equipment Emporium**. Other items may be available at the GM's discretion.

One notable item that is available from the vendors is **Glow Dust**. Sold in sticks like chalk, it is a colorful luminescent pigment that can be ground up and used to adorn one's body, or be blown through tubes to create glowing clouds. The dust will emit a faint but vibrant light for 30 minutes after being applied to a surface, longer for thicker coats. At the festival, its primary value is for amusement, but in a dungeon context, Glow Dust can be useful for tracing paths or blowing against walls and floors to detect irregularities (e.g. traps, secret doors).

Weapons and armor are strictly unavailable from any of the vendors.

Notable NPCs

With the exception of Vheld'broggn, the personalities listed below are friendly, or at worst indifferent, to the PCs.

Charmise, Human Thief 4: AC 14, #At 1 dagger, Dam 1d4+1, Mv 40', Ml 9, XP 400

HP 12 ☐☐☐☐☐ ☐☐☐☐☐ ☐☐

Charmise is the festival's Director. She is an entrepreneurial hustler and the whole event is a result of her vision and perseverance. Charmise is deeply in debt to the festival's sponsors and stands to lose everything if it is not a success. As the event

has been financed largely by the criminal underworld, this is no laughing matter. Charmise wears leather armor and carries a **Dagger +1** in her boot. She also has a magical **Necklace of Disguise** that allows her to assume the appearance (including the voice and mannerisms) of another creature once per day for up to two hours.

Grotzival, Elf Magic-User 6: AC 11, #At 1 dagger, Dam 1d4, Mv 40', Ml 9, XP 500

HP 18 ☐☐☐☐☐ ☐☐☐☐☐ ☐☐☐☐☐ ☐☐☐

Grotzival is the festival's Lighting and Audio Engineer. Famous for his innovative "wall of sound" projection technique and amazing synchronized illusions, he is a well-known and highly sought-after figure on the concert circuit. Securing his participation was a major coup on Charmise's part and a key factor in securing the investment needed to allow the project to go forward. Grotzival is confident to the point of arrogance and dedicated totally to the technical aspects of the show. He keeps his spell book under lock and key in his quarters.

Lieutenant Pete, Human Fighter 3: AC 15, #At 1 sword or club, Dam 1d6+1, Mv 40', Ml 9, XP 300

HP 20 □□□□□ □□□□□ □□□□□ □□□□□

Lieutenant Pete is Charmise's Chief of Security. A decorated veteran of several major military campaigns, he has retired from service and entered into in the lucrative world of private security. Lieutenant Pete is disciplined and loyal, if rather unimaginative. He wears chain armor and carries a short sword and club.

Jack, Human Child (age 9): AC 10, #At 1 fists, Dam 1d4, Mv 40', Sv NM, Ml 4, XP nil

HP 2 □□

Jack is Lieutenant Pete's squire and apprentice. He is a non-combatant and is always at Lieutenant Pete's side.

Elbor, **Furio**, and **Ron**, Human Fighter 1: AC 14, #At 1short sword or club, Dam 1d6 or 1d4, Mv 40', Ml 9, XP 100 ea.

HP 8 □□□□□ □□□
    8 □□□□□ □□□
    8 □□□□□ □□□

These three are members of Charmise's security detail. They once served under Lieutenant Pete, who recruited them to serve as muscle for his security consulting operation. They are equipped with leather armor and helmets, and wield short swords and clubs.

Drella and **Fitz**, Human Fighter 1: AC 14, #At 1short sword or club, Dam 1d6 or 1d4, Mv 40', Ml 9, XP 100 ea.

HP 8 □□□□□ □□□
    8 □□□□□ □□□

Drella and Lil Fitz are female members of the security detail. They are equipped as per Elbor, Furio and Ron. Underestimate them at your peril.

Chyken, Human Thief 3: AC 11, #At 1short sword or club, Dam 1d6 or 1d4, Mv 40', Ml 9, XP 100

HP 6 □□□□□ □

Ostensibly one of the female security guards, Chyken is actually a spy planted by the investors to keep an eye on Charmise. Grotzival suspects that there may be more to her than meets the eye, but otherwise no one has any reason to believe that she is anything but a professional and trusted member of the team. Chyken is equipped as per the other guards, but keeps a set of thieves' tools hidden on her person at all times. She also has a **Ring of X-Ray Vision** that she wears on a chain around her neck. Chyken will try to position herself near Charmise whenever possible, unless specifically assigned duties by Lieutenant Pete.

Jay Sylvanpool, Performer: AC 11, HD 1, #At 1 fists or dagger, Dam 1d4, Mv 60', Sv F1, Ml 12, XP nil

HP 7 □□□□□ □□

Sylvanpool is the missing performer the PCs have been engaged to locate. He is a true triple threat, famous for his acting, dancing and singing prowess and is known (by reputation) to everyone at the fair, including the PCs. In addition to his love of the arts, Sylvanpool is an antiquarian with a passion for exploring ruins. His curiosity got the better of him and despite the repeated warnings of the staff and clearly posted signage, he wandered off into the temple's lower levels where he is now lost.

Vheld'broggn, Extradimensional Abomination: AC 18, HD 25, #At 1 bite or miasma (see below) + 3 tentacles, Dam 2d8 or 1d10/1d10/1d10, Mv 90' Fly 60', Sv F20+5, Ml 12, XP 9,000

HP 125 □□□□□ □□□□□ □□□□□ □□□□□
        □□□□□ □□□□□ □□□□□ □□□□□
        □□□□□ □□□□□ □□□□□ □□□□□
        □□□□□ □□□□□ □□□□□ □□□□□
        □□□□□ □□□□□ □□□□□ □□□□□
        □□□□□ □□□□□ □□□□□ □□□□□
        □□□□□

Vheld'broggn manifests as a repulsive bipedal creature standing approximately eight feet tall. Its skin is blotchy and covered with a layer of bloody mucus, from which patches of wiry hair irregularly emerge. Where a head would normally be, it instead has a trio of tentacles surrounding a gaping maw; in lieu of arms are what can best be described as flaps resembling the body of a sting ray which it uses to fly. It has a variable number of eyes which seem to shift across the surface of its hideous body, blinking in and out periodically. The overall effect is utterly horrifying and any creature that beholds Vheld'broggn must successfully save vs. Spells or suffer the effects of the **confusion** spell for 2d4 rounds.

Vheld'broggn can attack with all three of its tentacles every turn. Each tentacle is 15' long and capable lifting up to 250 pounds. Vheld'broggn will grab a victim with the tentacles, pull the victim to its maw to rend and chew the victim to death, then regurgitate the bloody remains. Any creature struck by a tentacle must save vs. Paralysis or become ensnared. An ensnared creature may not attack or cast spells, but can attempt a subsequent save to escape, once per round.

If not actively devouring prey, Vheld'broggn can emit a potent miasma once every ten rounds through its maw that affects all creatures within a 30' radius. Any creature in range must save vs. Poison or become infected and take an automatic 5 HP damage per round until they are cured or die. If a save is successful, or if a target is cured, that creature is immune to further exposure to miasma for the next 24 hours.

Vheld'broggn's motives are as inscrutable as they are destructive. Its mentality and consciousness are so far beyond mortal comprehension that communication with it is all but impossible. It regards all living creatures as prey and thrives on the fear and the horror it creates in the minds of its victims as they die. Vheld'broggn consumes living creatures exclusively and will ignore the dead (or those that it believes to be dead). Whenever it kills, Vheld'broggn heals damage equivalent to the fatal strike.

Vheld'broggn is immune to all poison, as well as **sleep**, **charm**, or **hold person** spells. Any attempt to communicate with it telepathically will result in the total and permanent insanity of the contacting party.

Ironically the creature's weakness is music, which causes it to become distracted and suffer a -4 penalty on all attack rolls and -8 to AC while any music is being played within its range of hearing. It is up to the GM's discretion as to what would constitute such a performance, although Sylvanpool might be of assistance here. Once Vheld'broggn has identified a source of music, it will target it with its attacks exclusively until it is destroyed.

Vheld'broggn is not intended to be a fair opponent for the PCs. If they are unlucky enough to encounter it in combat, then they have failed to close the gate and are facing the consequences.

Upper Level Key

1. PORTICO:

> An imposing set of double doors, fifteen feet tall and banded with iron, separates the temple interior from the world outside. A pair of braziers on either side of the porch burn day and night to ward off the damp. Two sentries huddle under the roof of the porch, avoiding the drizzling rain.

Two of the NPC guards will always be stationed here and rotate throughout the day in 6 hour shifts. If the PCs are not yet known to the guards, they will summon Lieutenant Pete, who will escort them to area 3 to meet the Festival Director.

Close inspection will reveal that the doors are decrepit and hardly as sturdy as they appear from a distance; the left door is not attached to its hinges and is simply propped up against the frame. Disturbing the door will cause it to tip, causing 1d8+2 points of damage to anyone it lands on.

2. VESTIBULE:

> This large room was once the temple's vestibule and is bustling with activity. Festival staffers and performers hurry about "Discussing Business" and "Getting Things Done".
>
> The room has a tall vaulted ceiling and the remains of an intricate mosaic floor can be seen. A huge set of double doors, directly opposite the entrance, is closed.
>
> To the right, a smaller door is open and leads to a hallway, from which people seem to be coming and going.
>
> To the left a similar door is closed and marked with a sign reading "RESTRICTED AREA".

The vestibule area is tidy, but a close look at the walls and ceiling reveals its shabby condition.

PCs who eavesdrop or engage passers-by in conversation may learn of the following rumors:

1. The weather is really bringing everyone down. But the vendor's area is a bright spot – lots of stuff for sale.

2. The crowd is getting more and more worked up – the show had better be good or who knows what this many people could do.

3. There is some bad "brown wine" going around that is making people in the crowd sick.

4. Bits of mundane gossip about various performers (so-and-so is sleeping with so-and-so, so-and-so won't go on if there are any dwarves backstage, so-and-so's voice is giving out, etc.)

5. Grotzival's special effects are going to be over the top – this might be his best show ever.

6. The "thing in the other room" spoken in hushed tones with a furtive glance towards the double doors, referring to the apparition in area 14. Some think Grotizval is behind it, which he will (truthfully) deny.

7. Multiple people have had the same nightmare featuring a monstrous creature entering an underground room through an octagonal portal.

At night this area will be lit by braziers standing in each of the room's corners, but devoid of traffic.

3. OPERATIONS CENTER:

A sign on the door reads "MANAGEMENT ONLY". The room contains a large table surrounded by twelve chairs, occupied by people at work. Spread out across the table are ledgers, charts and diagrams. A chalkboard on the eastern wall is covered with lists and other writings. The area is busy, with staffers moving about and discussing the preparations for the festival.

Charmise sits at the head of the table and is engaged in conversation with one of her assistants. When the PCs are introduced she will dismiss all of the other staffers except for her Chief of Security, Lieutenant Pete.

By day, there is an 80% chance that Charmise will be found here. If not, she will be in either area 2, 4, or 5 working with staff or performers on matters related to the festival.

The documents on the table detail the festival's business operations. The writing on the chalkboard is a congeries of to-do items, scheduling concerns and notes regarding the upcoming events.

It is apparent that this room sees a lot of use, as there are overflowing ashtrays and half-finished coffee cups strewn about the table.

4. VIP LOUNGE:

Couches and cushions line the walls of this room, the floor of which is carpeted with a fine woven rug. Side tables arrayed with food and drink are situated among the couches and a table in the center of the room holds neatly arranged plates and glasses. A hearty fire burns in the fireplace at the rooms western end, driving away the chill.

This is a reception area for the festival's A-list performers and guests. The foods present include fruit, cheese, candies and other delicacies. Ale, wine and liquors of the highest quality are among the beverages.

During the day, performers and their entourages may be found here, enjoying the amenities. If the PCs engage them in conversation they may learn rumors as described in area 2.

5. UNUSED ROOM:

The door to this room is stuck and must be forced open. It opens into an empty, disused chamber covered in cobwebs and dust. The bones of small animals lie scattered about along with other detritus. A fireplace opposite the door has been bricked over.

If asked, the festival staff will mention that they couldn't open the door and thus did not use this room for any purposes. Should the PCs examine the fireplace, they will see that the mortar is crumbling and the bricks can easily be removed revealing a hollow space behind. Once enough bricks have been removed 6 giant cockroaches will stream through the opening and attack the PCs.

A search of the space will reveal the moldering, nearly skeletal remains of a Halfling. A crude map of the lower level along with 12 cp, can be found among the Halfling's bones. The map is now ruined and largely illegible, but a Thief that studies it for a full turn may learn of the secret door that leads to areas 18-21. How the unfortunate Halfling met his fate is unknown.

6 Giant Cockroaches: AC 15, HD 1*, #At 1 bite, Dam 1d4, Mv 30' Fly 60', Sv F1 (immune to disease, saves as C10 vs. Poison), Ml 6, XP 37 ea.

HP	8	☐☐☐☐☐ ☐☐☐	7	☐☐☐☐☐ ☐☐
	4	☐☐☐☐	4	☐☐☐☐
	5	☐☐☐☐☐	6	☐☐☐☐☐ ☐

6. STAIRWELL:

> The hallway ends with at door, with a large sign reading "DO NOT ENTER – UNSAFE AREA" written in Human, Halfling, and Elven script. The door seems to have been barred at one point but the beam has been pried off and is now leaning against the eastern wall. The door is now slightly ajar.

The door will open halfway without issue at which point it seizes and will not budge. The opening is wide enough for a human-sized character to squeeze through. If (when) the PCs open the door:

> The door opens to reveal a set of stone steps leading down into the darkness below. A layer of thick dust and debris from the ceiling covers the steps, but they are passable. A stale, musty odor emanates from the area below.

Close inspection of the steps reveals a set of footprints leading down, but none returning.

7. GUARDS' QUARTERS:

> This room has been converted into quarters for the Director's security detail. Three bedrolls lie on the floor and clothing and other personal effects are scattered sloppily about the room.

The guards Elbor, Furio and Ron (see page 39) have set up in this room. By day there is a 25% that one or more will be resting in here; otherwise they are out on patrol. By night they will all be here unless on guard duty in area 1.

Stashed amongst their belongings are three purses containing a total of 25 cp, a small mirror, a bottle of cheap cologne, a worn deck of playing cards.

8. GUARDS' QUARTERS:

> This room has been converted into quarters for the Director's security detail. It is neatly arranged, with a folding cot against the far wall and a bedroll on the floor next to it. A small table with a candle and inkwell sits between the cot and bedding.

Lieutenant Pete and Jack (see page 39) have taken over this room. By day, there is a 5% chance they will be here, otherwise they are with the Director. If they are absent, the door to the room will be closed and locked with an iron padlock. The two are always together.

The bed is tightly made and the room is well organized. A foot locker containing clothing, 15 sp and Lieutenant Pete's journal sits at the foot of the cot. The journal is unremarkable and mundane, consisting mostly of observations about the weather and staffing details. A PC who reads it will learn the names and number of guards and other festival personnel.

A second foot locker next to the bedroll holds clothing sized for a boy and a small box containing a set of lead soldiers and some dice.

9. GUARDS' QUARTERS:

> This room has been converted into quarters for the Director's security detail. Two bedrolls lie on the floor and a makeshift hammock hangs against the far corner. Various personal effects are scattered sloppily about the room.

Drella, Fitz, and Chyken (see page 39) are lodging in this room. By day there is a 25% that one or more will be resting in here; otherwise they are out on patrol. By night they will all be here unless on guard duty in area 1.

The remains of last night's dinner (chicken bones and stale heels of bread) sit on a table in the center of the room along with dirty plates and dishes.

Stashed amongst their belongings are a total of 75 cp, a homesick letter from Ron to his mother (that he believes lost and is frantically looking for, lest anyone else read it), and some cheap jewelry worth no more than 5 sp.

10. DIRECTOR'S QUARTERS:

> A small room with a cot and small writing desk. It is neatly arranged, and the bed is made and does not appear to have been slept in. An inkwell, blotter and small silver figurine of a ballerina sit upon the desk.

These are Charmise's quarters, but have seen little of her, as she has been working non-stop on festival business for the last few days. The figurine is made of silver coated brass mounted on a porcelain pedestal. It is a child's toy that will play music if wound up with a key. The figurine is of sentimental value to Charmise, and worth at most 3 cp if sold.

Under the cot and hidden in a crevice beneath loose stones in the floor, is a chest containing the festival's working cash. It contains 3,500 gp, 2,700 sp, 400 cp, and 50 emeralds, worth 20 gp each, in a pouch.

In the drawer of the writing desk are sheets of paper and a wax seal with her mark. Hidden behind the desk is a leather pouch containing the key for the figurine and correspondence between Charmise and festival's sponsors. A PC who finds and reads these letters will learn that the festival is backed by some heavy criminal elements and of how deeply in debt (in excess of 50,000 gp) Charmise is to them. When she flees on the final day, the pouch, chest and figurine will be gone.

11. ENGINEER'S QUARTERS:

> The wall of the room opposite the door is lined with makeshift shelving and a table fashioned from crates and boards, on which are stacked haphazardly various containers jars, reagents, beakers and other alchemical vessels. Along the northern wall is a bed and a small chest.

The door to this room has been **wizard locked** by Grotzival. The table and shelves contain the various ingredients and raw materials for his audiovisual magic. In the chest are a pouch holding 20 sapphires (worth approximately 500 gp), Grotzival's contract with Charmise and his spellbook. A PC who reads the contract will learn that Grotzival is paid a percentage of the festival's net after expenses, which seems like a dubious proposition to anyone with any business sense.

The spellbook contains the following entries: **charm person**, **magic missile**, **ventriloquism**, **magic mouth**, **continual light**, **wizard lock**, **ESP**, **phantasmal force**, **mirror image**, **levitate**, **dispel magic**, **fireball**, and **invisibility**.

12. TRASHED ROOM:

> The door to this room is unlocked but closed. In the center of the room are the remains of a large fire that has been apparently used to burn rubbish and garbage, which is scattered about the corners of the room. The room has a foul, close smell that makes one want to leave.

This room has been used by generations of visitors to the temple as a dump site. A cursory search of the remains of the fire will reveal nothing of value. Any PC who probes or stirs up the ashes must make a save vs. Poison or inhale some of the dust and be sickened (treat as affected per the **bane** spell) for 2d8-1 hours, or until they have rested for 8 hours, whichever occurs first.

13. WEAPON CLOSET:

> The door to this room is locked with an iron padlock. Inside stand two large racks, one holding eight sets of full chain mail; the other eight shields and eight pikes. To the right of the door are two small barrels. There are four crates on the floor in the western corner.

The barrels contain a total of 10 gallons of lamp oil and are labeled "FLAMMABLE". The heads of the pikes are silvered.

The crates hold various pieces of equipment including:

- A large tent (10 man)
- 4 crowbars
- 2 hammers
- 50 iron nails
- 10 iron spikes
- 200' of hemp rope
- One week of dry rations for 8 people
- Cooking tripod and large pot

The racks are warded with a **magic mouth**. If anyone but Lieutenant Pete or Jack touches or otherwise disturbs the equipment, it will begin screaming "ALARM!" until disabled. This will immediately attract the attention of the guards who will respond within 2 rounds, and will not be amused if they find the closet has been broken into.

Lieutenant Pete keeps the key to this room on his person at all times.

14. NAVE:

This was once the main area of the temple. An arcade with stone columns leads to an apse with a raised platform and stone altar. The floor and walls of the room must have once been covered with marble, but it seems to mostly been stripped. Stained glass windows above, now smashed, allow dim light to enter during the day.

The roof and wall has collapsed towards the northern end of the room, and the floor is covered with straw, guano and other debris.

A shimmering apparition hovers over the altar, bathing the room in an eerie light. The image contained therein is of an oddly shaped hourglass, with octagonal bulbs. Black sand slowly drains from the top chamber, which is mostly full.

The altar is set inside a circle containing a repeating octagonal pattern.

Initially the emanation is about 3' wide and 5' tall; it will gradually grow, increasing to its full size of 10' wide and 15' tall by the morning of the first day. Striking or swinging at the apparition will have no effect, apart from a momentary disruption of its visual output.

On return visits to this area, the GM should remark on the progress of time, referring to the accumulation of sand in the hourglass' lower half. It is, of course, tracking the approach of Vheld'broggn. A PC that studies the hourglass and takes measurements will recognize that the sand will run out approximately at sundown on the festival's final day.

Middle Level Key

While not visible from above, the PCs will find that the stairs leading down from area 6 are completely blocked by debris and rubble from a collapsed ceiling at the first landing, save for a small passage. If PCs choose to crawl through the passage, they must do so single file and it will take a full turn to move to the landing before area 15.

The party may spend 12 hours to fully clear the rubble, although at least one PC must crawl through to assess the amount of work involved. Subtract 1 hour of work for each additional NPC they enlist to help with the effort. Should the PCs invest the time to clear the passage, they will make a grim discovery: the remains of a centuries-old adventuring party killed in the tunnel's collapse. Their bodies and equipment have long since decomposed and rusted away, although a **Sword +1, +2 vs. Undead** and a sealed scroll case containing **Scrolls of Knock, Fireball**, and **Wizard Eye** will be found amidst their bones.

By noon of the third day, **rioters** seeking access to lower levels of the temple will have joined forces to clear the passageway and the area will be unobstructed thereafter. The above-mentioned items will have fallen into their hands or become lost at the GM's discretion.

The air in the middle level of the dungeon is stale, and it is clear that the area has not seen any (human) traffic for a very long time. The walls in the hallway are covered with frescoes depicting bizarre and sacrilegious scenes, including human sacrifice and all manner of horrible creatures, although the colors have faded over the centuries. A recurring theme in the frescoes is the presence of an octagonal frame through which monstrous creatures observe the scenes from afar.

A faint smell of smoke lingers over the entire level, and layers of soot and grime cover the walls and ceilings of every room in this level.

All doors on this level are unlocked, but stuck with age and must be forced open. Ceilings in the rooms and hallways are 12' high unless otherwise indicated.

15. SMALL CHAPEL:

> A door on the landing at the end of the rubble pile opens into a small chapel. A large marble reredos carved with intricate octagonal patterns occupies the entire wall opposite the door, before which stands a small marble altar table. Three ancient prie-dieux stand in a semicircle around the altar, decaying with age.
>
> On the altar are two large and heavily tarnished candelabra and an odd roundish object.

The candelabra have been knocked over and contain the withered stubs of candles. They are made of solid silver and of exceedingly fine workmanship. They are worth 500 gp if cleaned up and sold to a collector (as a pair, somewhat less individually).

Upon inspection the irregularly shaped object will be revealed to be a humanoid skull of indeterminate species. It is gilded and studded with ten finely-cut amethysts. Perhaps it was once used as a chalice. The gilding has oxidized but can be cleaned up. Such a macabre object will require a very specific buyer, but one could imagine it fetching 750 gp for its materials alone (regard the amethysts as being worth 30 gp each if removed).

16. TORTURE CHAMBER:

> The ceiling of this room emits a weird luminescence, bathing the entire area in a faint light. The air is hazy and has a dank, moldy smell.
>
> The remains of a large rectangular wooden table fitted with iron stands in the center of this room. Attached to the head and foot of the table are devices resembling winches, and chains hang from the ceiling around it.
>
> A small stone stove stands in the corner, and various iron tools are scattered about. A tall wooden box, once covered with leather but which is now peeling and rotten, stands against the far wall next to the opposite door.

This room was once a torture chamber where the cult inflicted abuses and outrages on the subjects of its unspeakable experiments. PCs who have some experience with interrogation or imprisonment will recognize the equipment for what it is.

The box was a torture device and if opened will be found to contain the skeletal remains of an elf. As the box is opened, the PCs will swear they can hear a distant moan.

Unlike the others on this level, the door to area 16a is ajar and opens freely.

16A. OUBLIETTE (UPPER):

> The dank smell seems to emanate from this small room. Water drips from above and the walls are covered with lichen and fungus. A large statue of a golden fish stands against the far wall, reflecting the pale light from the room outside.

The entire floor of this closet is a hidden pit trap. A secret door at the bottom of the pit connects to room 21.

The statue is an illusion, placed to lure the unsuspecting into the room. Behind the statue is a patch of **yellow mold** that will emit a cloud of spores covering the entire room and extending 10 feet into area 16 when the trap is triggered.

The distance from the top of 16a to the bottom is 30', and any creature unlucky enough to trigger the trap and fall will take 3d6 points of damage. The commotion will waken **Jiminy the Ettercap** in area 21, who may attempt to communicate through the secret door with any PCs in the pit.

Yellow Mold: AC can always be hit, HD 2*, #At 1 spore burst, Dam 1d8/round for 6 rounds, Mv 0', Sv NM, Ml 12, XP 100

HP 9 ☐☐☐☐☐ ☐☐☐☐

16A. OUBLIETTE (LOWER):

> The walls and floor of the pit are slimy with lichen and water running down from above. It has gathered into a pool with an unusual greenish color about 4' in diameter in the corner. The floor is otherwise clean of debris.

The pool is actually a **green slime** which will activate and attack two rounds after any creature enters the room. The walls are exceedingly slippery and any Thief who attempts to climb them must take a +25% penalty on the roll.

The oubliette is warded with an **anti-magic shell** (per the spell, treat as cast by a 12th-level Magic-User), which covers the entire area and extends to the top of the shaft.

Green Slime: AC hit only by fire or cold, HD 2*, #At 1 special, Dam special, Mv 1', Sv F2, Ml 12, XP 125

HP   8   ☐☐☐☐☐ ☐☐☐

17. BURN ROOM:

> A rusted and scorched portcullis bars entry to this room. Inside are piles of ancient charred wood, charcoal and ash. The walls, floor and ceiling are caked thick with soot, and stalactites of carbonization hang from the ceiling. The room smells strongly of stale smoke. An area in far right corner away from the door appears to be noticeably clean and free of debris.

The portcullis can be lifted partially to allow about 2' clearance beneath. It will not stay up on its own and must be held or propped open. Its bottoms are sharp spikes and any creature that it falls on will take 1d8 points of damage and 1d4 points of damage per round until freed.

The stalactites in the ceiling are actually 4 **Darkmantles**, which will drop as soon as the PCs make their way to the center of the room. Once they fall, the ash and dust on the floor will be stirred up creating a choking cloud. PCs in the room must save vs. Poison or suffer coughing fits, causing a minus -4 penalty on all attacks made in the room for 2 full turns.

Directly above the clean area, a trap door in the ceiling here is hidden (found as a secret door). The trap door is actually a kind of flue, once used to vent smoke into the upper areas of the temple for use in their evil rituals.

4 Darkmantles: AC 17, HD 1+2*, #At 1 constriction, Dam 1d4, Mv 20' Fly 60', Sv F1, Ml 7, XP 37 ea.

HP   8   ☐☐☐☐☐ ☐☐☐   7   ☐☐☐☐☐ ☐☐
        5   ☐☐☐☐☐   6   ☐☐☐☐☐ ☐

18. CONTEMPLATION CHAMBER:

> This room is empty save for rusted iron chains with manacles that are set into the walls at regular 5-foot intervals.

A PC that observes the placement of the manacles will notice a break in the pattern, an empty spot in the wall where the door to the secret room lies. PCs who inspect the manacles will find various graffiti carved in the stone near the floor, containing names (perhaps of prisoners), such as: "Glover was here" and "Halford". Other messages are more grim: "God Save my Soul" and "Forgive Us for What They Do."

The secret room connected to this area is a short corridor leading to an open 5' square pit. A set of iron rungs leads down 50 feet into the darkness, opening into a 10 foot cubical room with a trap door in the floor. It is this trap door that connects to room 17, above (which, perhaps somewhat confusingly, is below room 18).

Openings in the ceiling of the secret room were used to vent smoke from the fires in area 17 into the temple's apse in area 14. These openings are permanently sealed and impassable, although particularly loud sounds from the upper level may be heard through them.

The walls, floor, and ceiling of the secret room are covered with thick soot and residue of fire similar to area 18.

19. SUPPLY CLOSET:

The secret door leading into this room slides up into the ceiling. If the PCs discover and open the door read the following:

> This room appears to be have been used for storage. Moldering furniture, crates and clay jugs and pots of various sizes are piled up haphazardly. A large shelf piled with scroll tubes sits against the far wall.

Set into the frame of the door is a guillotine trap. A successful detect traps check on the door area will reveal the presence of a button that can be pressed while raising the door to disengage the guillotine. If the button is not pressed before the door is opened, the blade will fall as soon as a creature crosses the threshold for 1d12 points of damage, and the door will slam closed again. When the when door is closed, the blade is raised again, ready for its next victim.

If the PCs spend two full hours searching the room, they may take an inventory of its contents. The jugs and pots contain oils, liquids and viscera which have long since spoiled. One small crystal container stands out from the rest and contains two doses of **Potion of Gaseous Form.**

The shelves are filled with 40 scroll containers containing the records of the temple. They are incredibly brittle and will tend to disintegrate if unrolled. For each PC that tries to read the scrolls, roll 1d6, with "1" indicating that the scrolls remain intact, otherwise they crumble into dust. If a PC is successful at unrolling one or more, the contents may be read by anyone with an INT of 15 or higher. The language is archaic but appears to describe attempts to open a portal to a nether dimension.

Two containers are in better condition than the others. One contains a **Scroll of Neutralize Poison** and **Protection from Evil 10' Radius**, and the other a **Scroll of ESP**.

20. DISSECTION ROOM:

A polished stone table, approximately 8 feet long and 3 feet wide occupies the center of this room. It has gutters on the sides which open to drains in the floor below. Black stains mar the surface of the table, which is engraved with the octagonal motif common to the temple.

Sitting in one of the gutters is a sinister looking **curved dagger**. Although covered in dust, it is unusually shiny and seems immune to the general decay of the place.

A tiny square door (approximately 2 feet tall and wide) can be seen in a nook in the room's far corner.

The stains are from the gore of ancient victims and are still (strangely) tacky to the touch. The weapon on the table is a **Dagger +1** and is the one shown in various weird scenes. The PCs will recognize this immediately if they have seen it in one of these visions.

Apart from the table, dagger and usual dust and debris, this room is empty.

21. MONSTROUS CELL:

The small sliding door reveals a rectangular room covered with thick webs. Peering through the door you see what appears to be a sack near the far wall that has split open. Gold, silver and copper coins are scattered about.

Inside this room lurks Jiminy, a lonely Ettercap that has resided here for centuries. It has been ages since it has has a good meal and he is absolutely ravenous. Jiminy remembers entering through the pit in area 16a and knows of the secret door, but is unable to open it from this side. Alas the creature is too large to fit through the small door leading to area 20, so here he has remained, eking out a meager subsistence on such vermin that make the temple their home.

Once the door is opened (or if someone falls into the pit in area 16a), Jiminy will waken and eavesdrop on their conversation. He will keep himself out of sight, but attempt to lure them into the room by faintly calling for help. Jiminy knows nothing of Sylvanpool per se, but if the name is mentioned, he will discern that it refers to someone the PCs are interested in and attempt to play the role to trick them into entering the room.

Given the size of the door, the PCs must crawl through one at a time, and as soon as a creature is halfway through, Jiminy will strike.

At one point this room was used as a pen for the bizarre monsters the cult used in its operations. The small door slides to the side, and allowed for food to be passed in from the preparation area.

The sack visible through the door is completely rotten, but its contents are: 50 gp, 347 sp, and 180 cp. The bones and equipment of its owner (Jiminy's last good meal) are strewn about the floor nearby.

Jiminy (Ettercap): AC 14, HD 6+1, #At 2 claws/1 bite + poison, Dam 1d3/1d3/1d8+poison, Mv 30', Sv F6, Ml 7, XP 500

HP 28 ☐☐☐☐☐ ☐☐☐☐☐ ☐☐☐☐☐ ☐☐☐☐☐ ☐☐☐☐☐ ☐☐☐

Lower Level Key

The stairs from the middle level lead past the Burn Room to a closed door. This area is thick with dust, and if searched, a set of footprints will be seen leading into area 25 ahead. The tracks were left by Sylvanpool.

Unlike the middle level, the walls here are plain and unadorned. The smell of smoke is less prevalent and the area is generally dry and dusty. Ceilings in the hallways are vaulted at 10' intervals and 15' tall. Unless otherwise indicated, all doors are made of thick wood with iron bands and unlocked. However, they are all stuck with age and must be forced open. The noise from doing so will be noticed and attract nearby creatures. Once opened, a door will spontaneously slam shut after one turn and must be forced open again. The mechanism behind this effect is unknown.

22. FOYER:

> This room is empty save for the skeleton of a long-dead adventurer in the corner, clad in crumbling armor and still clutching a rusted sword. Several metal bolts lie scattered around the bones, and several are stuck into the wall behind.

A pressure plate in front of the skeleton will trigger a trap that fires six crossbow bolts from the opposite wall, causing 1d6 points of damage each. A PC that triggers the trap may save vs. Death Ray for half damage. Unless deactivated by fixing the plate, the trap will trigger three more times before its supply of ammunition is exhausted.

The skeleton's equipment is long since ruined, but it has 15 gp, 12 sp, and 4 cp in a rotten leather pouch.

23. WORKROOM:

> Broken furniture and collapsed shelves clutter this room. Among the junk a tarnished but otherwise intact golden brazier stands out.

In the bowl of the brazier is small octagonal frame made from a strange black metal. These objects are the same ones from the weird scenes and will be immediately recognizable to the PCs if they have seen them in one of the illusions.

The brazier is magical and, when lit, will make visible any magic within a 30' radius, per the spell detect magic. This feature may be used once per day, but will last until the fire burns out. If the brazier is moved while lit, the effect will travel with it, but will fail if the brazier is spilled or otherwise extinguished. The octagonal frame has no magical powers, but its metal is extremely unusual and will require the assistance of a sage to identify. As such it may have value to wizards or alchemists.

If the PCs search through the detritus for a full hour, they will uncover an ornately carved wand that seems to have escaped the ruin of the other objects here. It is a **Wand of Fireballs** with one charge remaining.

24. VAULT:

> The door to this room is made of iron with three keyholes and a large handle. It is locked and will not budge.

The locks on the door are normal, if ancient. A Thief that attempts to pick the locks must make separate checks for each one. If the PCs manage to open the door, read the following:

> Recessed shelves line the walls of the rear half of this small room. The shelves are somehow illuminated, providing a dim light. Most are bare, but a long case and several small jars remain. Two large crystal statues flank the shelving area and glimmer in the eerie light.

This room is a vault that once held the precious objects used by the cult in its rituals, and the crystal statues are its guardians. If the command phrase ("Timoteo Sent Me") is not spoken within one minute of opening the door, the statues will animate and attack anyone who enters. They will not leave the room and will try to close and lock the door once any intruders have been expelled.

The most valuable items were removed when the site was abandoned, but certain objects were left behind that might be useful in the event of the temple's reactivation. The long case contains a **Spear +1** with the power to **locate objects** in the temple area once per day. If the spear is removed from the temple, it will permanently lose this feature. The jars contain 1 **Potion of Control Undead** and 1 **Potion of Cure Disease**.

2 Living Statues, Crystal: AC 16, HD 3, #At 2 fists, Dam 1d6/1d6, Mv 30', Sv F3, Ml 12, XP 145 ea.

HP 15 ☐☐☐☐☐ ☐☐☐☐☐ ☐☐☐☐☐
   15 ☐☐☐☐☐ ☐☐☐☐☐ ☐☐☐☐☐

25. EMBALMING ROOM:

> Two stone tables, each supporting a 6 foot marble slab, fill the center of this room. In the corner diagonal from the door is a small brick oven. The far wall once held shelves of jars, bottles and other containers but have collapsed with age and scattered their contents across the floor.

The tables have gutters similar to those in area 20.

The footprints from area 22 seem to lead up to the wall opposite the door and stop. Disturbing the debris under the collapsed shelves will cause a pack of rats to emerge and attack the party.

All of the containers have been smashed or are empty and their contents long since disintegrated. Inside the oven is charcoal and ashes of ancient matter, but nothing of value.

Pack of 35 Rats: AC 11, HD 1 hp each, #At 1 bite/pack, Dam 1d6+disease, Mv 20' Swim 10', Sv NM, Ml 5, XP 360 (pack)

Each checkbox represents one rat.

HP 35 □□□□□ □□□□□ □□□□□ □□□□□
        □□□□□ □□□□□ □□□□□

26. LABORATORY:

> Broken glass covers the floor of this room, in which stand three large tables with steel surfaces. The air here is much colder than the surrounding rooms, and PCs who enter can see their breath. Two glass jars containing a gray substance sit on the center table, and an ancient pair of leather gloves sits beside them. All four walls are streaked with a strange black substance, that seems to have been spattered on and run down.

This room was once used as a cold lab for the cult. It is warded with magic that keeps the temperature at a constant 40° F (~4° C). The two jars contain gray oozes in suspension. At the room's low temperature they are dormant, but if handled (or brought out of the area) the warmth of a PC's touch will activate them, causing them to expand and shatter the jars in 1d4 rounds.

The black goo on the walls is blood and is sticky to the touch.

2 Gray Oozes: AC 12, HD 3*, #At 1 pseudopod, Dam 2d8, Mv 1', Sv F3, Ml 12, XP 175 ea.

HP 15 □□□□□ □□□□□ □□□□□ □
    12 □□□□□ □□□□□ □□

27. SECRET CORRIDOR:

> The secret door leads into a small corridor. The ceilings here are lower than those of the surrounding areas (approximately 5 feet tall), and the air is especially stale and dusty. Thick cobwebs hang from the ceiling. The corridor has a dirt floor, and the walls are lined with brick. Timber beams support the walls and ceilings.

Sylvanpool is trapped here. He entered through the secret door in room 25, but his torch went out shortly afterwards and he has been unable to find the door through which he entered. If he hears activity in rooms 25, 26, or 32 he will loudly call for help. Such noise will waken the crypt dwellers in area 32, who know of the secret door and will be drawn to it.

28. ANTECHAMBER:

> The hallway widens into an antechamber, with two doors on its northern wall. A hallway at the western end turns to the south. Two wooden benches fill the expanded area, making it seem like a waiting room of some time. The floor is tiled with black stone arranged in a now familiar octagonal pattern.

The room is otherwise empty.

29. SACRISTY:

> Wooden closets and cabinets cover the walls of this room, and a small basin stands in the corner. A bench sits against the wall to the right of the door, and pieces of a smashed table lie in its center. Two clay cups sit on a ledge next to the basin.

The drawers and closets are filled with the rotten remains of the vestments, robes and other outfits worn by the cultists during their rituals. The cabinet on the western wall is rotten and any PC who attempts to open it will cause it to topple over, causing 1d6 points of damage to anyone beneath it. The clothing is worthless and heavily decayed, but searching through the drawers will reveal what once were the hooded purple robes seen in the various weird scenes.

The basin has two brass spigots, which are covered with corrosion and tarnish. If a PC turns the right spigot, it will emit a slow stream of brown, brackish water. The left will a dark red, strong-smelling liquid that appears to be blood; this will dry after a few minutes. If the blood and water are mixed together and consumed, they will form a **Potion of Vitality** that grants 1d10+2 temporary hit points for 2d6 turns. When the effect wears off, the imbiber will be left with the lesser of his or her current HP or the HP he or she had at time time the potion was consumed.

30. BAPTISMAL POOL:

> In the center of this room stands a circular pool ten feet in diameter, whose sides rise about two feet off of the floor. The rim of the pool is made of discolored limestone, which is streaked with iron and calcification. Into its sides are carved strange writing in an unknown script. The water in the pool is thick with algae.

The air in this room is humid and damp. Small drops of water fall periodically into the pool and can be heard down the hallway and (faintly) into area 28.

The inscriptions in the side of the pool are written in the lost language of the cult. The PCs will not be able to read them except by magical means. If translated they say: "The drowned are not lost but float eternally downward in the black depths of Forever."

If the PCs skim the algae off the top of the pool, and probe the murky waters, they will find it to be four feet deep (2' below the surface of the floor). The bodies of three human children dressed in white robes (ages 1 to 3, completely preserved) lie in the muck at the bottom, with eyes open staring at the party.

Each PC that meets their gaze must save vs. Spells or be compelled to retrieve the bodies from the pool. Once brought to the surface, the bodies will rapidly decompose and dissolve into a repulsive, caustic substance. Any PC that handles or comes into contact with it takes 1d4+2 points of damage from the foul ichor.

31. GARGOYLE CLOSET:

The door to this room is a large stone slab with an iron ring for a handle. As the PCs pass it read:

> A large granite slab engraved with the image of a demonic creature, with horns and large wings is set into the wall. It holds out one taloned hand into which an iron ring has been mounted.

The door can be pulled open using the handle. It is a one-way door that can be opened from the hallway with ease, but not from inside the room without magical assistance. If the PCs open the door read the following:

> The door opens to reveal a small chamber, 10 feet square. On a pedestal in the center stands a stone statue of a demon resembling the image engraved in the door. Behind the pedestal appears to be an open box full of coins.

The statue is in fact a gargoyle and will attack any party members that enter the room. It will remain motionless until the PCs are within melee range, in order to surprise and inflict the most damage. The creature knows of the one-way nature of the door, and if it fails a morale check it will attempt to close the door as it flees, trapping the party in the room.

1,900 cp, 1,300 sp, and 600 ep can be found in the chest.

Gargoyle*: AC 15 ‡, HD 4**, #At 2 claws/1 bite/1 horn, Dam 1d4/1d4/1d6/1d4, Mv 30' Fly 50' (15'), Sv F6, Ml 11, XP 320

HP 21 ☐☐☐☐☐ ☐☐☐☐☐ ☐☐☐☐☐ ☐☐☐☐☐
☐

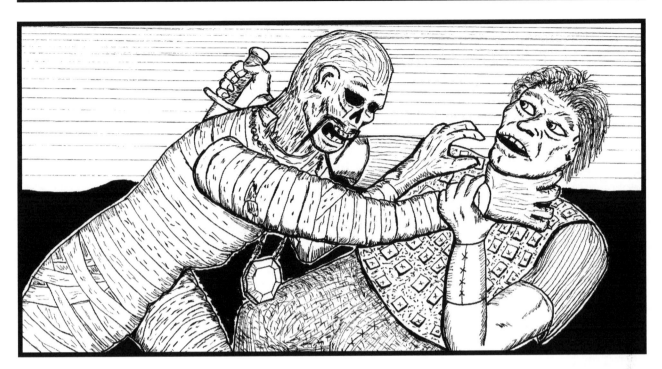

32. MUMMY CHAMBER:

> This room is empty save for a stone ledge about two feet off the ground running the length of the western wall. On the ledge rests a man-sized object wrapped in rotten linen. A red stone pendant on a golden chain is wrapped around what appears to be the object's neck. Two decomposing bodies sit on the floor propped up and facing the door as if on display. Between the two figures is a small stone box engraved with an octagon symbol.

Timoteo's mummy and the bodies of two of the cult's sacrificed members have been unceremoniously deposited in this room. Around the mummy's neck hangs the ruby pendant seen in various weird scenes. The PCs must approach the mummy to fully discern it, but will recognize it immediately if they have seen it in one of these visions.

The stone in the pendant is not glowing (as seen in the illusions) while worn by the mummy, but it radiates a strong magic. Once a PC obtains the pendant and hangs it around his or her neck, it will begin to glow. While the pendant is being worn, it will add an immediate +2 to CON and slow the aging of its wearer to the rate of 1 year for every 5 years of elapsed time. However if the pendant is ever removed, this benefit will vanish and the wearer will immediately and permanently age double the amount of time that the pendant was worn. For example, if worn for a year, the wearer will instantly age two when it is removed. A PC who dons the pendant will have a strong aversion to taking it off (treat per the **geas** spell) and resist any attempts to forcibly remove it.

The stone chest contains coins totaling 1,200 sp, 800 ep, and 2,600 gp. Once any creature comes within 5' of the mummy or crypt dwellers, they will awaken and attack.

Timoteo, Mummy: AC 17‡, HD 5**,
#At 1 touch+disease, Dam 1d12+disease, Mv 20',
Sv F5, Ml 12, XP 450

HP 23 □□□□□ □□□□□ □□□□□ □□□□□ □□□

2 Crypt Dwellers: AC 13‡, HD 2*, #At 2 claws or dagger, Dam 1d4/1d4 or 1d4, Mv 60', Sv F2, Ml 12, XP 100 ea.

HP 11 □□□□□ □□□□□ □
   10 □□□□□ □□□□□ □

33. GRAND HALL:

Two passages lead into this hall, each with its own door. Regardless of which the PCs choose, describe the passage as follows:

> A stone staircase descends into a chamber approximately twenty feet below. The walls of this passage are painted with depictions of vile monsters and unspeakable obscenities. Although faded with time, they are still recognizable and cause a feeling of unease. The room below is lit with an odd pulsating light.

If the PCs choose the left door, they will find a stairs leading into the hall below as described. If they choose the right, they will find a similar staircase, but one whose middle step is trapped. As soon as a PC places his or her weight on that step, the entire staircase will collapse into a slide and send the party careening down into the room below. Strands of razor thin wire cover the doorway on the lower end. Each PC on the stairs when the trap is activated will take 1d6 points of falling damage, and the first three PCs will take an additional 1d4 points of damage as they are lacerated by the wire rolling into the room. The wires will break and the stairs will reset themselves once the party has been deposited in the chamber below.

Once the party has made it into the area, read the following:

> The floor of this room is tiled with black stone. Rows of pews separated by a central aisle are arranged before a large stage with a podium at the far end. Behind it, an enormous, glowing distortion swirls, filling the chamber with an unnatural light. The air is hazy and smells of sulfur and decay. Amorphous figures seem to be present in the thing and fade in and out of view.

Once the PCs regain their bearings, they will notice that the pews are actually filled with an audience of the damned, observing the approach of Vheld'broggn. Fifteen skeletons sit patiently, awaiting its arrival.

The swirling apparition on the far wall is the gate, and the strange thing seen within is Vheld'broggn itself, although its full form can not yet be apprehended. If PCs observe the anomaly, it should be described as an unnatural shape that seems to be getting closer. Repeat visits to the area will confirm this observation.

15 Skeletons: AC 13, HD 1, #At 1 sword, Dam 1d6, Mv 40', Sv F1, Ml 12, XP 25 ea.

HP			
8 □□□□□ □□□		8 □□□□□ □□□	
8 □□□□□ □□□		7 □□□□□ □□	
7 □□□□□ □□		7 □□□□□ □□	
7 □□□□□ □□		5 □□□□□	
5 □□□□□		5 □□□□□	
5 □□□□□		4 □□□□	
4 □□□□		4 □□□□	
3 □□□			

Ending the Adventure

There are two general ways for the adventure to conclude: either the PCs will figure out the clues and devise some way to close the gate, or they will face Vheld'broggn in battle.

Vheld'broggn is a serious opponent and will almost certainly require support from the NPCs to defeat. If it is vanquished or the gate is closed, the madness will be lifted and the crowd will return to what passes for normal, forgetting all of the violence of the previous days. The weather will clear, Sylvanpool will give a legendary performance and the show will go down in the history books.

If the PCs manage to close the gate before Charmise disappears, she will reward them with the treasure in her room (knowing that she will more than make it up on the back-end and merchandising rights) and be able to repay her investors. If not, they will be paid only with the satisfaction of a job well-done. The backers of the festival, however, will be very interested in finding Charmise, and might be willing to hire the PCs to find her...

New Monsters

Flashbag

Armor Class:	10
Hit Dice:	1 hp
No. of Attacks:	1 explosion
Damage:	blindness
Movement:	20'
No. Appearing:	2d6
Save As:	Fighter: 1
Morale:	12
Treasure Type:	None
XP:	25

A **Flashbag** is a softly glowing orb that resembles a light inside a translucent membrane. They are non-intelligent, traveling in packs or flocks, floating gently if aimlessly around a given area. Flashbags are incredibly delicate, and can be destroyed with as much as a touch. Doing so will cause a noiseless explosion with a radius of 15' that causes no damage, but emits a brief, blinding light. Any creature that beholds the explosion must also save vs. Death Ray or be blinded for 2d4 turns. Given that they occur in groups, such an explosion is likely to cause a chain reaction, detonating any other flashbags in range, each requiring its own separate blindness save. Casting **darkness** on a flashbag (or its surrounding area) will inhibit the blinding effect of its explosion.

Awful Offal

Armor Class:	13
Hit Dice:	2
No. of Attacks:	1 bile spit/secretion
Damage:	1d8
Movement:	20'
No. Appearing:	1d4
Save As:	Fighter: 2
Morale:	12
Treasure Type:	None
XP:	75

A disgusting heap of viscous organ matter and entrails, an **Awful Offal** is the unnaturally animated remains of a humanoid that has somehow been separated from its skin and skeleton. Awful offals secrete a disgusting bile which they can spit up to 30', causing 1d8 points of acid damage and dissolving any organic matter it contacts (particularly wood) in 1d3 rounds. Striking an awful offal with a melee weapon will cause it to split into two separate creatures, each with half the hit points of the original. Such creatures may be further divided by subsequent blows until an awful offal has 1 HP, after which point any further damage will kill it. Awful offals take half damage from ranged weapons and full damage from any slivered weapons, neither of which cause the creature to divide.

Temple of the Seas

by Alan Vetter

Introduction

Centuries ago the Temple of the Seas offered a sanctuary for the people in the area that worshiped the old gods of the waters (The god of the oceans, the lower gods and goddesses of the seas, the gulfs and the rivers). The temple was on a high promontory with stairs leading down to a quay. As ships passed the captain and crew would stop at the quay, climb the stairs and make an offering for safe passage.

Over time the old gods fell out of favor and the temple was forgotten as the new religions took over. After a while the old captains died off and the new captains that had converted to the new religions stopped coming to the quay and the gods of the waters caused a storm to wash away the rotted quay and destroy a large portion of the stairs. Since the temple was dedicated to the gods of the waters there are no landward trails or roads leading to it.

Recently a sage, Tomas ("toeMASS") Redding, studying the old religions found references to the temple in old documents. Tomas has called on the adventuring party to investigate what is left of the building and what types of offerings, documents, or ancient religious texts are still at the temple.

The documents found by the sage stated the followers of the old gods were heretics and the leaders of the new religion had sent a crusade of "believers" to route the heretics and destroy the heretical building. Tomas would like the party to find anything relating to what beliefs the old religion taught, including especially any texts on the subject.

What Is Going On?

In the days when the temple was at its peak, a sea dragon lived in the lowest level of the dungeon (area 33). The leader of the temple (priest or priestess, for the followers of the god of the sea might be of either gender) would present the dragon as an avatar of the sea god. Anyone receiving a particularly significant blessing (and thus making a similarly significant donation) would be introduced to the dragon in a special ceremony by the temple leader.

The temple, being a holy place devoted to the god of the sea, had good relations with tribes of deep ones who lived (and still live, in fact) in the area. The deep ones had great respect for the sea dragon and had its permission to make use of the submerged entrance.

It happened that most of the crew of a merchant ship came down with a case of pinkeye. The captain brought his ship to the temple to make an offering in hopes of a cure, which of course the priestess would be happy to perform.

Had things gone according to plan, the priestess would have used a **cure disease** spell on the captain, then have him change into a white robe. She would have led the captain to the lower sanctuary for a ceremony in which he would give his offering to the sea dragon. The priestess would go through a long and complicated introduction in Draconic language, telling the sea dragon about the captain and the ship, and that he had brought a gift of friendship. This was done to prevent the dragon from attacking ships; the dragon would not attack the captain of a ship that had formally been introduced.

But even as the stricken crew members waited (in area 4) while the captain and priestess performed a ritual cleansing (in area 5), enemies were at the doors. Crusaders belonging to a new, fast-growing religion (possibly a precursor to the religion of the player characters) entered the temple, attacking the acolytes, the crew members, and eventually the priestess and captain. They were zealots, so sure the old religion was heresy that they threw down their weapons after bloodying them on the temple occupants, considering them unclean.

They were preparing to descend into the dungeon in search of additional followers, but they were unable to open the door to the stairs as they could not find the key. Their distaste for the "unclean" followers of the old sea god prevented them from immediately searching the body of the priestess, and so they had not yet discovered it when the earthquake hit.

Whether the earthquake was the retribution of the gods, or merely an unfortunate coincidence, did not matter to the crusaders. They fled to their ship at the quay below the temple, only to be crushed by falling rocks. The docks were destroyed as well, as was the unattended merchant ship. The crusaders had attacked that ship first, killing the few crew members who had not contracted the disease and had thus remained aboard.

The earthquake also collapsed the roof of the upper sanctuary (area 14) and caused the submerged entrance to the dragon's lair (area 33) to collapse. The dragon tried to get out, but as she entered the submerged cavern a large boulder fell on her, ending her life and leaving her single hatchling Ruhigisee an orphan. The deep ones helped the young orphan dragon survive but also helped themselves to some of her mother's treasure hoard. As a result she is cordial to the deep ones but learned long ago not to trust them.

The crusaders were drawn to the temple after one of the acolytes spoke to a few of the crusaders; they interpreted her statements of faith as an attempt to convert them, and in their outrage swore to destroy the temple. She fled to save herself, only arriving at the temple after the crusaders were there, and thus avoided the fate of the other temple occupants.

In the wake of the killings and the earthquake, this last acolyte transformed herself into a treant (by means she will claim to have forgotten) to save what was left of the temple and watch over it. She will be found apparently holding up the ceiling in area 14, below.

Holy Symbols Are Key

In several places in this adventure, tidal wave pendant holy symbols are mentioned. These are circular silver medallions about four inches in diameter with reliefs (raised symbols) depicting a tidal wave. This symbol is depicted below:

Many of the doors are marked with this symbol, reversed and relieved (cut into the door) so that the pendants will fit perfectly into the cavity. These doors are magically held as if by a form of **wizard lock** (which is resistant to **knock**) and can be opened easily by pressing a wave holy symbol pendant into the relief. All such doors lock again by magic if closed, and if left open but not spiked

or otherwise blocked they will slowly close of their own accord.

In some places a holy symbol or marking is described for the crusaders; their symbol was in the form of the head of a trident. No image is provided for this, but it may be described by the Game Master as needed.

Dungeon Level 1

1. PORTICO:

The columns at the front entrance are weathered statues of the gods and goddesses that were worshiped in this old decimated building. The double doors are warped and jammed in place, the lock on the doors is rusted to the point where the two halves are rust welded together. These double doors have a hardness of 8 and HP of 16.

> The columns here are actually statues in low relief holding up what is left of the entrance. The statues seem to have been hacked at with hammers or axes, with more damage visible lower down. Special attention was paid to the faces which are almost totally destroyed.

Behind the columns along the walls there are a number of weapons rusted beyond any use.

2. NARTHEX:

The noise of breaking down the doors has drawn two skeletons with swords.

> Once the front doors are broken in there are two skeletons waiting to attack anyone that tries to enter.

Once the skeletons are defeated the GM can read the description.

> Beyond the front doors is another set of double doors with a carving of a being rising from the ocean carrying a large trident and wearing a crown of coral. In the waves around the being are images of whales breaching, the whales are very small compared to the being that is rising from the oceans. On the horizon of each door is an image of a large wave.

There are single doors to the left and right. The door on the left has a sigil, resembling a tidal wave, the wave strongly resembles the waves on the double doors.

The door to the right is secured with an ordinary kind of lock; the key found with the priestess in area 5 will open it.

The door on the left with the tidal wave sigil on it will not budge and doesn't have a keyhole for a thief to try and pick. It is opened with a tidal wave holy symbol as described in **Holy Symbols are Key** on page 55.

The skeletons don't have keys for the two side doors. Neither skeleton has anything that would seem to match the design on the left hand door or the double doors.

If a thief unlocks the right door or the door needs to be chopped or broken down use hardness 8, HP 8. The hallway beyond is dark since there are no windows. The hallway beyond the door goes for 50' then turns left and goes for another 30'. There is a door on the left in the first section of hallway and one on the left and one at the end of the second section.

Murals on the walls depict many species of what seem to be fish; the fish that are shown are normally from the far deep (angler fish, giant sea horses and ore fish are examples).

2 Skeletons: AC 13, half damage from edged weapons, 1 point only from arrows, bolts, and sling stones, HD 1, #At 1 shortsword, Dam 1d6, Mv 40', Sv F1, Ml 12, XP 25 ea.

HP   8 ☐☐☐☐☐ ☐☐☐   7 ☐☐☐☐☐ ☐☐

3. FIRST OFFERING ROOM:

If asked the walls of this room show pleasant pastoral images with a river as the centerpiece of the image.

In the first section of hallway is a door on the left it has been broken off its hinges and hangs open. Beyond is a floor mat in the middle of the room laying before a cold fireplace. The mat has a large reddish-brown stain.

There is nothing left but cold ashes in the fireplace. The stain on the mat is dried blood, as might be

expected, though verifying this is left as an exercise for the players.

4. SECOND OFFERING ROOM:

The room to the left at the end of the second section of hallway. This room has a number of enhanced skeletons (see **Skeleton, Diseased** in the **Basic Fantasy Field Guide Volume 3**).

This is the largest of the offering rooms and there are actually several mats before the fireplace and several skeletons cover the floor. Among the skeletons are rusty weapons long forgotten, slightly curved swords and short spears for the most part.

If the party enters:

As the last person crosses the doorway the bones begin to come together.

Five of the skeletons were the crew of sailors who had stopped at the temple to make an offering when the building was attacked by the crusaders; the sixth, normal skeleton was an acolyte.

They are the owners of the weapons which were found outside the entrance. Weapons were not allowed into the temple itself; those found in this room were dropped after the crusaders had "defiled" them with the blood of the heretics. The pommels of the weapons carry a holy symbol of the newer crusader's religion. The crew and acolyte were attacked during their offering ceremony; they have become revenants, seeking revenge on any living beings who disturb their rest. The skeletons will ignore the weapons on the floor.

The crew had an outbreak of pink eye and were at the temple to make offerings for forgiveness to try and heal the disease. The crew skeletons have pink lights in their eye sockets. There is a 10% chance of party members catching the disease if they are hit for damage or if they touch the skeletons (such as punching or wrestling with them). The effects of the disease (blindness) will begin after 2d12 turns. The disease can only be cured by a **cure disease** spell.

Once the skeletons are dealt with players looking around will see the murals show different sea shore images of ships at docks and people fishing from piers. One of the skeletons, the normal one, has a

necklace with a pendant in the image of a tidal wave (one of the holy symbols described in **Holy Symbols are Key** on page 55).

The door in the wall to the right is locked.

Skeleton: AC 13, half damage from edged weapons, 1 point only from arrows, bolts, and sling stones, HD 1, #At 1 punch, Dam 1d6, Mv 40', Sv F1, MI 12, XP 25

HP   7   ☐☐☐☐☐ ☐☐

5 Diseased Skeletons: AC 15, half damage from edged weapons, 1 point only from arrows, bolts, and sling stones, HD 2, #At 1 punch, Dam 1d8 + disease (pink eye), Mv 40', Sv F2, MI 12, XP 75 ea.

HP   7   ☐☐☐☐☐ ☐☐   5   ☐☐☐☐☐
     3   ☐☐☐   2   ☐☐
     3   ☐☐☐

5. THIRD OFFERING ROOM:

After the door is unlocked from the second offering room:

> Two skeletons lie on a mat of woven reeds in this room. They don't seem to be animated; they just lie there, reassuringly dead. The clothes rotting on their bones seem finer than the that worn by the skeletons in the previous room.

This is the captain and the high priestess; he was dressed in a ceremonial brown robe, while she was wearing a dark blue robe with yellow embroidery similar to the one in the armoire in room 7, below.

The captain was the leader of the crew in the previous room. They were in here for a more specialized ritual that only the captain of a ship was privy to. The murals here show ancient cities that seem to be underwater. There is a necklace with a key and a tidal wave pendant (one of the holy symbols described in **Holy Symbols are Key** on page 55) on the priestesses bones. The key unlocks the basement stairs (room 6) and the door to the right hallway in room 2, as well as the door to this room (though it does no good as the adventurers must have already picked or broken that lock).

6. STAIRS TO THE BASEMENT:

The door is at the end of the right-side hallway. It is locked and trapped with a poison needle. The poison is no longer lethal but, will cause 2 points of damage and -2 to hit checks for 2 turns. The trap is so old that even if the key is used the trap will go off.

> A set of dusty stone steps lead down to the darkness. The steps go down 20' then turn left and go down another 10'. At the bottom of the steps there is a door and the open stairs continue again to the left.

The door at the bottom of the stairs is to room 15; see Level 2 below. The hallway murals extend down all the stair wells.

7-13. DORMITORY AREA:

The left hallway runs 30' then turns right and extends another 60'. There are doors every 20' across from each other in the hall.

> There are no murals on the walls of this hallway; it appears it was whitewashed at one time but shows every indication that decades have passed since then; the walls are patchy and dingy. There are sconces on the wall but they are empty and long disused.

7. PRIESTESS' QUARTERS:

The first door on the left side of the hallway is for the room of the high priestess. The door is locked and trapped with a poison needle. The poison is no longer lethal, but will make a person that springs the trap ill. The needle will do 1d3 points of damage if a saving throw vs. Poison fails, and only a single point if the save is made. The affected party member suffers an AB penalty of -1 for the next 2 turns.

> As you enter this room you see a bed to the left, and at the foot is a chest. To the right stands a desk and an armoire. A piece of paper lies on the desktop, with a quill lying beside it and an open ink bottle nearby.

The bed is made, but the woolen blanket is moth-eaten and the bedding stiff and stale-smelling.

Inside the chest are tunics and undergarments which belonged to the priestess. Inside the armoire are the dry rotted remains of several robes, dark blue in color with bright yellow embroidered wave designs along the hem, cuffs, and collar. In the desk are dried out ink bottles and several yellowed sheets of paper.

The paper on the desk is the start of a letter from the high priestess to her mother. She explains that her new assignment is going well and that she is about to have her first captain's ceremony at this temple with the captain of a boat that just came in. The letter is unfinished, and the ink bottle is completely dried out and useless.

In the bottom drawer of the desk are 4 sp, 5 ep, 7 pp, a 50 gp blood-stone, a 100 gp piece of alexandrite, and a 10 gp amethyst.

Under the bed is a **Shortbow +1** wrapped in a linen sheet; it does not have a string, and will need to be restrung before it can be used.

8. LEAD ACOLYTE ROOM:

This room is across the hall from the Priestess' room. The door is locked but not trapped.

> There is a bed and chest to the left. There is a desk across from the door.

The bed is made but the material has long since rotted. The chest contains tunics, trousers, and a single dark blue robe, all neatly folded. At the bottom are 10 gp wrapped in a scrap of cloth.

9. ACOLYTE ROOM:

The door to this room is not locked.

> There is a bed and chest on the right side of the room, and a desk stands against the wall across from the door. Lying in the bed is a skeletal corpse with a dagger stuck in its ribs.

Like the other acolyte rooms there is a bed and a chest. In the chest are tunics, trousers, a blue robe and a pouch containing 18 sp and 2 gp. The desktop is empty but in the single drawer is an ink bottle (stoppered, but still dried out), a quill, and a pile of papers. On top of the pile is an unsent letter; it is addressed to someone named Esmond and tells that a new high priestess is coming and questions how she will work out. The signature is illegible, so the writer's name remains unknown.

There is a tidal wave holy symbol (one of the holy symbols described in **Holy Symbols are Key** on page 55) in the chest.

The dagger has the religious symbol of the crusaders embossed onto the pommel.

10. ACOLYTE ROOM:

The second door on the right is unlocked.

> There is a bed and chest on the left side of the room, and a desk stands against the wall across from the door. The bed is made but the bed linens are tattered and rotten.

There is nothing at all in the chest.

11. ACOLYTE ROOM:

The third door on the left is locked.

> Lying on the bed to your right are two skeletal figures, pinned together with a broken spear. At the foot of the bed is a chest, and a desk stands against the wall across from the door. Scattered beside and partially under the bed are articles of clothing, robes and slippers and undergarments by the look of it, and two bronze medallions with cracked leather thongs lie on the desk as if thrown there.

Two of the acolytes were having a tryst when the crusaders stormed in and put a spear through the both of them; it broke, so the crusader left it. The neck of the spearhead has the same holy crusader symbol as the one in Room 9 and any other weapons found inside the temple.

There are 18 sp and 16 gp in the bottom of the chest, under an assortment of neatly folded masculine clothing.

The medallions on the desk are tidal wave holy symbols as described in **Holy Symbols are Key** on page 55.

12. ACOLYTE ROOM:

The door of this room is ajar; it squeals somewhat, but not very loudly, when opened.

> There is a bed on the left side of the room, and a desk stands against the wall across from the door. The bed frame is bare, and what is left of the mattress is rolled up at the foot of the bed. You don't see a chest here.

Other than the items described, this room is empty.

13. ACOLYTE ROOM:

After the door is unlocked at the end of the hallway:

> There is a bed straight ahead of you, a chest in the diagonal space to your left, and a desk to the right. The bed isn't made, and the bed linens are tattered and rotten.

There are a number of rats in this room since the original occupant had hidden food in a corner. The food has long since rotted to nothing, but the rats have a nest here.

In the chest are the usual tunics, trousers, and robes, but they are rudely piled inside, not folded like the ones in the other rooms.

In the single drawer of the desk is the usual paper, quill, and ink bottle (dried up like the others) as well as a letter written in a sloppy hand. It is addressed to someone named Nesta, and in it the writer complains about the hierarchy bringing in another high priestess from far away, and questions why the author of the letter had not been picked to lead the temple. The writer also mentions being contacted by people that were not believers in the sea gods, and how, if successful, this acolyte could bring them into the fold. The letter is unfinished.

At the bottom of the chest are 14 sp, 16 ep, 14 gp, 18 pp, a 600 gp bowl, a 1,100 gp tiara, and a **Scroll of Protection from Lycanthropes**.

17 Normal Rats: AC 11, HD 1 HP, #At 1 bite per pack, Dam 1d6 + disease, Mv 20'/Swim 10', Sv NM, Ml 5, XP 10

Each checkbox represents one rat.

HP 17 ☐☐☐☐☐ ☐☐☐☐☐ ☐☐☐☐☐ ☐☐

14. SANCTUARY:

Each of these doors has the tidal wave symbol carved into it; as with the left-side door of area 2, they are locked magically and can only be opened using the tidal wave pendants as described in **Holy Symbols are Key** on page 55. However, for these doors **two such holy symbols** are needed to open them; neither door will open unless both are unlocked.

> As with the columns of the portico, the columns here are statues in low relief, damaged in the same way as those columns and thus barely recognizable as ancient gods and goddesses. The last statue was actually so destroyed that it fell. A section of the wall has fallen in at the back of the dais and a tree is growing in the open space with branches supporting the remains of the roof. Floor mats lie scattered on the floor throughout the room.

At the dais a section of the wall has collapsed and a tree is growing in the open space. **Any party member who steps onto the dais** will hear a voice asking if they are believers or not. If the party answers "yes" or "no" the treant releases the roof and attacks the party.

Once the treant is down to less than 10 HP she will try to parlay; she only wants the party to leave. She will tell her story more or less as given on page 54 in **What's Going On?** It has been centuries since she has had to speak Common and so her speech will seem rather archaic. If asked why she attacked, she will reply that since the party is armed she thought they were another group of crusaders.

The treant protects the temple and the scrolls that were commonly read in the sanctuary. The scrolls have long since rotted away, leaving the rollers bare. There are only a few scraps of the original text, nothing that could be used to recreate it. The treant would be happy that the old religion has not been totally forgotten, but will be saddened to hear that it is no longer practiced.

The walls were painted at one time with scenes of ships in a storm, ships on calm waters, and ships that are docked. One panel seems to depict a sea dragon attacking a ship.

Treant: AC 19, HD 8*, #At 2 fists, Dam 2d6/2d6, Mv 20', Sv F8, MI 9, XP 945

Note: Treants normally can animate nearby trees to assist them in combat; however, no trees are nearby which can be animated, so no statistics are given for such assistance.

HP 58 □□□□□ □□□□□ □□□□□ □□□□□
      □□□□□ □□□□□ □□□□□ □□□□□
      □□□□□ □□□□□ □□□□□ □□□

Dungeon Level 2

15. STORAGE CLOSET:

The door is not locked but it has swollen shut. Once it is forced open read the text box.

> This is a storage closet for the priestess or acolytes to continue to the rest of the catacombs. There are a number of dried out torches in a barrel and some brooms and mops used to clean the temple and the catacombs when the temple was actually in use.

If one of the players pull a torch out of the barrel they will disturb the Yellow Mold at the bottom of the barrel. The mold will blow it's spores out of the top of the barrel. Roll an attack on any characters standing next to the barrel.

Yellow Mold: AC can always be hit, HD 2*, #At 1 spore burst, Dam 1d8/round for 6 rounds, Mv 0', Sv NM, MI 12, XP 100

HP 9 □□□□□ □□□□

16. PRE-BURIAL RITUAL ROOM:

Past the previous door the stairs continue down another 30'. The open stairs end at another platform with a door to the right and more steps going down to the left again.

> A set of dusty stone steps lead down to the darkness. The steps go down 30' then turn left and keep going down into the dark. To the right is a door that is locked.

The door can be opened with one of the tidal wave pendants.

> The room has a table to the right (in the alcove). There is a coffin on the top of the table. Under the table is a wooden box.

This room was used by the temple hierarchy to prepare bodies for burial in the rest of the catacombs. The body of the deceased was put into the coffin and left to decay. Once it was down to just bones the skeleton was put into the wooden box and then stored in one of the rooms of the catacombs beyond this room. There is a lair of giant cockroaches behind the box under the table. These cockroaches eat the flesh of the recently deceased, thus helping the decaying process; the temple personal didn't know about them. The giant cockroaches are rather hungry and attack.

8 Giant Cockroaches: AC 15, HD 1*, #At 1 bite, Dam 1d4, Mv 50', Sv F1 (immune to disease, saves as C10 vs. Poison), MI 6, XP 37 ea.

HP 1 □   5 □□□□□
    5 □□□□□   5 □□□□□
    2 □□   6 □□□□□ □
    3 □□□   4 □□□□

16A. ENTRANCE TO CATACOMBS:

The small room appears to be a closet, but nothing seems to be stored here. The floor of the room slowly drops 30'. Make a secret door check to see if the player finds the door. If the door is not found after a round the floor will go back up and reset for the next person to descend.

17. MIDDEN:

From room 16 the left hallway goes down for 30' then turns left for 120', another left turn and another 30' down and a second left, and another 30' feet down. There is a stuck door, and to the left even more stairs going down into Level 3. Once the door is opened read the following:

> Beyond the door is a curtain of metallic beads.

The beads are statically electrified; anyone that touches it will receive an electric shock for 4d6 points of damage (see the **lightning bolt** spell in the **Basic Fantasy RPG Core Rules**).

> Past the bead door is a large room with a low rail in one corner. Past the rail is a 10' deep pit; if anyone looks down into it that person may see glints of gold and silver.

Anyone that looks into the pit must make a roll on INT to see the additional glint from the gelatinous cube at the bottom of the pit. If anyone looks up they will see a hole in the ceiling over the pit.

Gelatinous Cube: AC 12, HD 4*, #At 1 slam, Dam 2d4 + paralysis, Mv 20', Sv F2, MI 12, XP 280

HP 9 ☐☐☐☐☐ ☐☐☐☐

If the gelatinous cube is defeated players will find 14 sp, 20 ep, 10 gp, a 10 gp topaz, a 50 gp greenstone, a 50 gp bloodstone, and a 500 gp phenalope.

If the group is in the room longer than a turn the metal ball curtain will be recharged.

18. PRIEST AND PRIESTESS' BURIAL CHAMBER:

The door is not locked or trapped.

> The room is lined with boxes of bones and some bodies that appear even older and are wrapped in cloth.

Former priests and priestesses that passed away are stored in this room. Among the boxes of bones are some older burials that are actually mummies. These mummies arise and pick up weapons after the last person enters the room.

There is a leather bag with 1,700 sp, 1,400 gp, and a 1,000 gp brooch made of gold with a rounded ovoid (egg-like) shape, set with a spiral pattern of tiny pale lavender sapphires.

There is a secret door found on a 1 on 1d6. Beyond is a short hall of 10'; the end actually comes out in a 10' hole in the floor. If anyone falls in the hole they will fall 70' onto the gelatinous cube in room 17.

The walls of the rooms 18 to 21 are all whitewashed. There is some dirt on the walls but it appears this was dust from some other experience.

3 Mummies: AC 17‡, HD 5**, #At 1 touch + disease, Dam 1d12 + mummy rot, Mv 20', Sv F5, MI 12, XP 450 ea.

HP 17 ☐☐☐☐☐ ☐☐☐☐☐ ☐☐☐☐☐ ☐☐
    29 ☐☐☐☐☐ ☐☐☐☐☐ ☐☐☐☐☐ ☐☐☐☐☐
        ☐☐☐☐☐ ☐☐☐☐
    21 ☐☐☐☐☐ ☐☐☐☐☐ ☐☐☐☐☐ ☐☐☐☐☐
        ☐

19. SECRET STORAGE:

The door to this room will be found on a 1 on 1d10; since it is actually just a half door, the bottom is about 4' above the floor. This is a well-hidden treasure trove of the scrolls that document the tenants of the older religion of the temple. A certain sage may pay handsomely for these scrolls (3,000 gp).

Just outside the door for Room 20 is a hallway that ends at a secret door. The latch to open the door is very obvious from this side. This comes out in the middle of the 120' hallway between Rooms 16 and 17.

20. ACOLYTE BURIAL ROOM 2:

The doors are stuck, but not locked. This smaller room was for the lead acolytes that had died in service to the temple.

> There are many boxes of bones in this small room.

The bones will assemble into skeletons to protect from looters. If a member of the party is wearing a necklace with the tidal wave pendant, the skeletons will not attack and will return to their boxes. If no one is wearing the pendant or just carrying it the skeletons will attack, assuming the person carrying the pendant has stolen it.

There are 8 skeletons; 4 will get up at a time and attack.

8 Skeletons: AC 13, half damage from edged weapons, 1 point only from arrows, bolts, and sling stones, HD 1, #At 1 punch, Dam 1d6, Mv 40', Sv F1, Ml 12, XP 25 ea.

HP	6 ☐☐☐☐☐ ☐	5 ☐☐☐☐☐
	6 ☐☐☐☐☐ ☐	1 ☐
	5 ☐☐☐☐☐	6 ☐☐☐☐☐ ☐
	2 ☐☐	8 ☐☐☐☐☐ ☐☐☐

21. ACOLYTE BURIAL ROOM 1:

The door is stuck. This room was for the regular acolytes that had died in service to the Temple.

> There are many boxes of bones in this small room.

The bones will assemble into skeletons to protect from looters. If a member of the party is wearing a necklace with the tidal wave pendant, the skeletons will not attack and will return to their boxes. If no one is wearing the pendant or just carrying it, the skeletons will attack assuming the person carrying the pendant has stolen it.

There are 8 skeletons here; 4 will get up each round and attack.

8 Skeletons: AC 13, half damage from edged weapons, 1 point only from arrows, bolts, and sling stones, HD 1, #At 1 punch, Dam 1d6, Mv 40', Sv F1, Ml 12, XP 25 ea.

HP	8 ☐☐☐☐☐ ☐☐☐	5 ☐☐☐☐☐
	8 ☐☐☐☐☐ ☐☐☐	4 ☐☐☐☐
	6 ☐☐☐☐☐ ☐	4 ☐☐☐☐
	1 ☐	8 ☐☐☐☐☐ ☐☐☐

Dungeon Level 3

22. ENTRANCE TO LOWER SANCTUARY:

From Room 17 the stairs continue down 10', turns left and drops another 20', and ends at a locked door. **The door at the bottom of the stairs is locked** and will need a tidal wave pendant to open. If the party needs to break it down use Hardness 8, HP 8.

This lower level has been overrun by a group of Deep Ones; more information can be found in the **Basic Fantasy Field Guide Volume 2**.

Most corridor areas on this level have been whitewashed recently enough that a faint sour odor still lingers in the air. Area 27 has not been visited by Deep Ones and is not whitewashed.

> When you open the door you see two humanoids that look more like fish than men.

If the door was bashed down the deep ones will be at the ready, if a pendant was used roll for normal surprise (1-2 on 1d6).

The hall and stairway painting motif of sea creatures continues into this room. There is another pendant-locked door in this room.

2 Common Deep Ones: AC 16, HD 3+3, #At 2 claws or scimitar, Dam 1d4/1d4 or 1d8, Mv 20' Swim 30', Sv F3, Ml 8, XP 145 ea.

HP	14 ☐☐☐☐☐ ☐☐☐☐☐ ☐☐☐☐
	20 ☐☐☐☐☐ ☐☐☐☐☐ ☐☐☐☐☐ ☐☐☐☐☐

23. PRIESTESS' STUDY:

Outside the second door of room 22 are two hallways: one going straight ahead the other to the right. The hallway to the right is about 90'. There is a T-intersection after 50' leading to the left. The murals end here and go on to the hallway to the left. Straight ahead is another formally white-washed hall ending with a door on either side. If someone listens at the door on the right, he or she will hear a snoring noise. There is a sigil on this door to use the pendant. If the players bash in the door (Hardness 8 HP 16) the two deep ones in this room have time to get up and prepare for battle. If a pendant is used the two deep ones are asleep. Roll for surprise or have the Thief roll to Move Silently into the room. Determine surprise and then run the rest of the fight.

If the door was bashed in:

> The door comes down and another two fish-looking people stand ready with swords.

If a pendant was used to open the door:

> The door opens and on the floor are two fish people snoring loudly.

After the fight the characters will see that this looks more like an office than a bedroom; it was the priestess' office at one time. There is a desk shoved against the wall and a broken chair. In the drawers of the desk are papers concerning the acolytes; one is noteworthy as saying that an acolyte may have to be transferred since she was belligerent to the former priest and was heard making disparaging remarks about the new priestess.

If the bodies are searched one of them has a key on a necklace. The necklace could be worth 1,300 gp.

2 Common Deep Ones: AC 16, HD 3+3, #At 2 claws, Dam 1d4/1d4, Mv 20' Swim 30', Sv F3, Ml 8, XP 145 ea.

HP 26 ☐☐☐☐☐ ☐☐☐☐☐ ☐☐☐☐☐ ☐☐☐☐☐
☐☐☐☐☐ ☐
20 ☐☐☐☐☐ ☐☐☐☐☐ ☐☐☐☐☐ ☐☐☐☐☐

24. WATER CLOSET:

Across the hall from the Priestess' Office is another door that isn't locked.

> There is a bench in the alcove to the right. The bench has a hole in the top about a foot in diameter.

This was the water closet, or restroom, for the priestess and acolytes. If anyone looks down the hole they will see a gray mass at the bottom of a 10' deep pit. The gray mass is actually a small gray ooze that was used to keep the waste of this privy disposed.

Gray Ooze: AC 12, HD 3*, #At 1 pseudopod, Dam 2d8, Mv 1', Sv F3, Ml 12, XP 175

HP 10 ☐☐☐☐☐ ☐☐☐☐☐

25. DINING HALL:

The door to this room from the corridor is open. Anyone approaching will hear sounds of feasting, including loud conversations in an unknown low-pitched language. **The room is illuminated** by four torches, each in a sconce in the center of a different wall. **The secret door is opened** by pulling outward (away from the wall) on the sconce in the center of the north wall.

Going straight from the second door in room 22 is a whitewashed hall going 40', after 30' the hall has a T going to the left for another 30'; an open door is on the right at the end of the hall.

In the whitewashed room are six of the deep ones sitting at what is left of the table.

> As you enter you see the horror of the fish-looking men feasting on what could only be the remains of a merman.

Unless the adventurers are extremely loud, the feasting fish-men will not be aware of them, so surprise should be rolled. The kitchen staff will come after 1d6 rounds if there is much more of a commotion than what the deep ones were making while eating.

> This is a dining room, furnished with very old and rickety-looking furniture that nonetheless somehow held up to the fish-man feast.

The secret door in the corner can be found like a common secret door. See room 27 if this corridor is found.

6 Common Deep Ones: AC 16, HD 3+3, #At 2 claws or shortsword, Dam 1d4/1d4 or 1d6, Mv 20' Swim 30', Sv F3, Ml 8, XP 145 ea.

HP 13 ☐☐☐☐☐ ☐☐☐☐☐ ☐☐☐
13 ☐☐☐☐☐ ☐☐☐☐☐ ☐☐☐
17 ☐☐☐☐☐ ☐☐☐☐☐ ☐☐☐☐☐ ☐☐
18 ☐☐☐☐☐ ☐☐☐☐☐ ☐☐☐☐☐ ☐☐☐
18 ☐☐☐☐☐ ☐☐☐☐☐ ☐☐☐☐☐ ☐☐☐
16 ☐☐☐☐☐ ☐☐☐☐☐ ☐☐☐☐☐ ☐

26. KITCHEN:

At the end of the hall from room 22 is a door that is shut, but not locked. If someone listens they may hear the sounds of pots banging inside the room.

> Opening the door reveals two of the fishy-looking creatures cleaning the pots in the kitchen.

Roll for surprise since the deep ones were not expecting intruders and were busy with their work. After 3 rounds check to see if the deep ones in the dining hall (room 25) come in, if they have not been dealt with yet. They have long knives available which are equal to daggers and thus not as effective as their dual claw attacks; however, if they are drawn to the fight in room 25 they will take their knives for throwing if that appears to be a good strategy.

Once the deep ones are dealt with, the party will see this is a kitchen and is still being used as one. Although the deep ones are not as neat as regular humanoids would be.

In the back corner is a secret door found like normal; see room 27 if this corridor is found.

2 Common Deep Ones: AC 16, HD 3+3, #At 2 claws or dagger, Dam 1d4/1d4 or 1d4, Mv 20' Swim 30', Sv F3, Ml 8, XP 145 ea.

HP 20 ☐☐☐☐☐ ☐☐☐☐☐ ☐☐☐☐☐ ☐☐☐☐☐
   16 ☐☐☐☐☐ ☐☐☐☐☐ ☐☐☐☐☐ ☐

27. WELL:

The deep ones have not found this secret hallway which was once used by the acolytes on kitchen duty to go between the kitchen, dining hall, and the pantry.

> This corridor is not whitewashed as the others on this level have been. You can see two other secret doors, which are obvious from the back side, and an open alcove with a low-walled well with a crank mechanism above it; a bucket hangs there, suspended by a blackened chain speckled with rust.

If anyone takes a drink from the well that character will get the benefits of a 4th-level **water breathing** spell (8 hours).

28. LOWER NARTHEX:

Coming off the T-intersection from the hall between rooms 22 and 23, the hallway widens into this room outside the lower sanctuary.

> The murals go around the room and up to the two doors. The image on the doors seems familiar.

The image on the doors is a mirror image of the doors going into room 14. They are opened with two pendants also.

The hallway continues on for another 20' before turning left 10' to a locked door (Hardness 8 HP 8). It uses the same key as the one for the stairs, room 6, and to the right hand hallway from room 2.

29. MAIN LIBRARY:

If the door is broke down the four deep ones in this room will be ready for a fight. If the key is used roll for surprise as normal.

If door is bashed down read this:

> As the door falls off the hinges, four fishy-looking humanoids attack.

If the key is used read this:

> The door opens and you find four of the fishy-looking men bent over a small table, which appears to have dice and coins on it.

If the key is used roll for surprise before running the fight. If the door was bashed in just run the fight.

Once the deep ones are dealt with the players will see that this was once a library. After a round of searching through the remaining bookshelves, the players could find a set of books that are just the book spines that cover a small chest. The chest is trapped with a poison needle. The key to the chest can be found on the leader in room 23. In the chest are 4,300 gp, a **Shield +2**, a **Cursed Scroll**, and a **Rod of Cancellation.** If anyone looks at the cursed scroll roll 1d6; the character will lose 1d4 points from an Ability Score. Use the order from the **Basic Fantasy RPG Core Rules** to determine the number: STR = 1 to CHA = 6. A save vs. Spells will stop the curse from happening. An affected character needs to have a **remove curse** cast on him or her to start recovering from the effects of the scroll.

4 Common Deep Ones: AC 16, HD 3+3, #At 2 claws or scimitar, Dam 1d4/1d4 or 1d8, Mv 20' Swim 30, Sv F3, Ml 8, XP 145 ea.

HP 15 □□□□□ □□□□□ □□□□□
17 □□□□□ □□□□□ □□□□□ □□
16 □□□□□ □□□□□ □□□□□ □
16 □□□□□ □□□□□ □□□□□ □

30. LARDER:

Before the turn to room 29 there is a secret door which can be found as usual. Beyond the door is another 30' of hallway. At 20' is a hallway branching to the left and one branching to the right at the end. The right-hand hall way goes for 40' and ends at a doorway. The door is locked, but the key to the other areas of the temple will open this door. If the players break-in the door (Hardness 8, HP 8) the two deep ones in this room have time to get up and prepare for battle. If the key is used the two deep ones are asleep. Roll for surprise or have the Thief roll to Move Silently into the room. Determine surprise and then run the rest of the fight.

If the door was bashed in:

> The door comes down and another two fish-looking people stand ready with swords.

If the key was used to open the door:

> The door opens and on the floor are two fish people snoring loudly.

After the fight the players will notice that there are shelves and racks attached to the ceiling that have heavy nasty-looking hooks. This was at one time the larder for the temple; meat was hung on the hooks in preparation for being cooked and served to the acolytes. Any meat that was in here before is long since gone.

2 Common Deep Ones: AC 16, HD 3+3, #At 2 claws or scimitar, Dam 1d4/1d4 or 1d8, Mv 20' Swim 30, Sv F3, Ml 8, XP 145 ea.

HP 16 □□□□□ □□□□□ □□□□□ □
15 □□□□□ □□□□□ □□□□□

31. BROOM CLOSET:

The hallway to the left described in the larder room goes for 30'; there is a door to the right, then it goes for another 20' and ends in another door. The first door is not locked.

> Inside this small room are cleaning implements and supplies for the lower level of the temple, mostly brooms and mops with badly rotted heads.

Other than the items described, there is nothing of interest in this room.

32. PANTRY:

The door at the end of the hallway is locked. **If anyone listens** they may hear a grunting noise from the room beyond. The key works for this door too. If the players break in the door (Hardness 8 HP 8) the two deep ones in this room have time to get up and prepare for battle. If the key is used the two deep ones are under a blanket. The deep ones are making enough noise that they will not notice the door opening. You may roll for surprise or allow the Thief to roll to Move Silently into the room. Determine surprise and then run the rest of the fight.

If the door was bashed in:

> The door comes down and another two fish-looking people stand ready with swords.

If the key was used to open the door or the secret door from Room 27 was found:

> The door opens and on the floor are two fish people under a blanket making a loud moaning noise.

When the party is able to search the room, they will find that it is lined with shelves and barrels. This was the pantry for the kitchen.

> This appears to be a pantry; there are empty shelves and barrels all around the room.

At the bottom of one of the barrels is a false bottom, found as a secret door. In the open area under the false bottom there are 1,900 sp, 4,100 gp, and 19 pieces of jewelry. The jewelry includes two 1,200 gp anklets, a 1,400 gp belt, three 1,300 gp bowls, a 1,500 gp brooch, a 600 gp brooch, a 900 gp brooch, a 1,100 gp buckle, a 700 gp choker, a 300 gp clasp, a 1,400 gp crown, a 1,200 gp flagon, a 1,100 gp goblet, a 900 gp goblet, a 900 gp pin, a 600 gp plate, and a 1,000 gp statuette.

2 Common Deep Ones: AC 16, HD 3+3, #At 2 claws or scimitar, Dam 1d4/1d4 or 1d8, Mv 20' Swim 30', Sv F3, Ml 8, XP 145 ea.

HP 16 □□□□□ □□□□□ □□□□□ □
    14 □□□□□ □□□□□ □□□□

33. LOWER SANCTUARY:

The doors from room 28 are much like the doors to the Sanctuary (Room 14). As the party descends the stairs 20' to the main sanctuary, there is a sunken section of floor 20' beyond where the room opens; the sunken section is flooded. There are column statues going down either side of the room extending out into the flooded floor.

After the double doors from room 28 are opened there is a grand staircase going down 20'; the room opens out into a large grotto. As the room opens up there are two more steps going down to a flooded section of floor. There are eight statues that are also columns; these statues have not been destroyed like the ones in the sanctuary upstairs.

If the party searches past the last columns they will find a large gray beast with wings sleeping, or at least pretending to be asleep if the party has made any noise.

If the party wishes to parlay the dragon will speak in a very archaic Common. The dragon will explain that she has always lived here. At the far back of the sanctuary is a section of floor that opens underwater into a cave, the original entrance her mother used for this lair. Many years ago when she was just a hatchling, the entire sanctuary shook, as explained on page 54 in **What's Going On?**, leading to the collapse of the

@sketchingjohn

submerged entrance cave. If the party looks into the cave they will see the skeleton of a dragon, its head crushed by boulders.

The deep ones were able to get through the cave and bring her food. They raised the orphan dragon, but didn't teach her that she could fly, and since she saw her mother die in the collapse she has not been down in the lower cave. The dragon did discover that she could breathe steam and was able to use that weapon. The parent dragons had a good-size hoard but the deep ones demanded payment for the food they brought the dragon and so have taken some of it.

Note that the relationship between the dragon and the deep ones is thus on a "transactional" basis. She is not their friend nor ally, unless they choose to pay her for her services just as they make her pay for food.

The dragon will pay the party handsomely if they are able to clear a path for her to get through the tunnel, or provide some other way to exit the dungeon. It should take 32 hours of mining for eight humans to get through the cave-in; if there is a dwarf in the party the time can be reduced by four hours for each dwarf that works on the project, to a minimum of 16 hours.

If the dragon is freed she will give a quarter of her remaining hoard to the party. The hoard includes 3,200 cp, 21,000 sp, 20,000 ep, 26,000 gp, two 1,000 gp anklets, a 800 gp bracelet, a 1,100 gp brooch, three 700 gp buckles, a 600 gp buckle, a 1,300 gp chain, a 500 gp choker, three 900 gp combs, a 400 gp earring, a 900 gp earring, two 1,500 gp goblets, an 800 gp knife, three 1,000 gp lockets, a 2,000 gp scepter, and an 800 gp statuette. The jewelry and art total 21,300 gp.

Ruhigesee (Sea Dragon, age level 6): AC 19, HD 10*, AB +9, #At 2 claws/1 bite or breath, Dam 1d8/1d8/3d8 or breath, Mv 10' Fly 60'* (20') Swim 60' (15'), Sv F10, Ml 8, XP 1,015

HP 45 ☐☐☐☐☐ ☐☐☐☐☐ ☐☐☐☐☐ ☐☐☐☐☐
☐☐☐☐☐ ☐☐☐☐☐ ☐☐☐☐☐ ☐☐☐☐☐
☐☐☐☐☐

Farin's Folly

by Clinton L. Robison

Introduction

Many years ago, Priest Farin, a Cleric of good, grew tired of the adventuring life and migrated to the area to preach the gospel to the locals. Farin proved to be even better with his words than with his mace and soon had gathered a small group of disciples.

Before long the small group of disciples had grown into a congregation. Farin believed a congregation needed a place to worship and began construction on a temple overlooking the sea. The temple was a glory to behold, and soon people journeyed from neighboring villages to worship at Farin's shining temple.

However, this all soon went to Farin's head and before long he began to delude himself into believing that his spells and miracles were all his own, not the benevolence of his god. Soon even his congregation began to believe Farin a deity.

Farin, unknown to his followers, had actually been influenced by a deep one known as Vriruh. Vriruh sought to use Farin's cult as a source for both food and research into a way to contact his dark gods. Vriruh also despises humans and took great pleasure in corrupting Farin's mind.

Farin's one-time deity did not approve of Farin's newfound "godhood." Farin's temple was struck with the forces of nature, and Farin himself and many of his followers cursed to undeath.

For the GM

This is a potentially deadly adventure. A well-balanced party is recommended, but extra spellcasters wouldn't hurt. Magical items and healing spells and items are essential to surviving, even if the party decides to take this adventure in multiple attempts.

Adventure Hooks

The GM may wish to create certain reasons for the PCs to be interested in journeying to Farin's Folly. Ideas for adventure hooks include:

- Local villagers have told tales of seeing ghostly figures near the old temple at night.

- Legends that Farin's cult existed beyond his death (or even that Farin himself still lives).

- The old priesthood is interested in restoring Farin's Folly to a useful temple again and hire the PCs to investigate.

Upper Level Key

1. PORTICO:

> As you approach the temple steps, the ornate stone columns leading to the doors grab your attention. They seem to have once been gleaming marble columns, but are now faded and covered in overgrown greenery which extends across most of the steps as well.
>
> The doors just on the other side of the vegetation lie open and barely attached to the walls.

While most of the columns are covered in ivy and other vines, the two columns closest to the doors are actually covered by assassin vines. The assassin vines will surprise the adventurers on a roll of 1-4 on a d6. They will attack quickly as they are eager for a meal bigger than squirrels and birds.

2 Assassin Vines: AC 15, HD 6, #At 1 + special, Dam 1d8 + special, Mv 5', Sv F6, MI 12, XP 500 ea.

HP 12 ☐☐☐☐☐ ☐☐☐☐☐ ☐☐
      19 ☐☐☐☐☐ ☐☐☐☐☐ ☐☐☐☐☐ ☐☐☐☐

Treasure: 10 sp and 4 cp are scattered about from previous victims of the vines.

2. FOYER:

> The once gleaming white stonework of the foyer is now tarnished and gray. A group of giant rats scurry about, looking for a place to hide.
>
> The doors ahead and to the left hang open in a similar fashion to the doors to the temple. To the right the door appears shut tight.

The giant rats are eager to escape a fight, but will retaliate if the players attack first.

5 Giant Rats: AC 13, HD 1d4 hp, #At 1 bite, Dam 1d4 + disease, Mv 40', Sv F1, MI 8, XP 10 ea.

HP 4 ☐☐☐☐   4 ☐☐☐☐
      1 ☐   3 ☐☐☐
      4 ☐☐☐☐

3. ACOLYTE'S STUDY:

The door to this room is locked.

> As soon as you open the door, you are set upon by two heucova.

The heucova were Clerics in training under Farin. They are a result of the curse that was laid upon Farin and his followers. They have no spells prepared. Both carry a mace, but will attack with claws first.

2 Heucova: AC 16†, HD 2**, #At 2 claws or 1 weapon, Dam 1d4 claw or by weapon, Mv 40', Sv C2, MI 10, XP 125 ea.

HP 15 ☐☐☐☐☐ ☐☐☐☐☐ ☐☐☐☐☐
    9 ☐☐☐☐☐ ☐☐☐☐

Treasure: 5 gp, 1 gem (worth 56 gp).

> The room appears to be a relaxing study for priests in training. Any furnishings once here have since rotted and broken away. A fireplace against the wall looks to have been recently disturbed.

The fireplace is trapped with some sharp barbs. If the PCs fail to detect the trap they trigger the barbs and take 1d2 points of damage. The fireplace contains 8 gp and a **Dagger +1**.

4. FARIN'S STUDY:

> This room appears to have once contained several bookshelves with books and scrolls. The furnishings have now crumbled. There are also several sets of bones littering the floor and one assembled skeleton lying near the fireplace.

The various bones are four skeletons with a skeletaire lying by the fireplace. As the adventurers approach the fireplace the skeletaire will stand up and command the skeletons to rise up and attack the players, followed by casting **darkness**.

4 Skeletons: AC 13, HD 1, #At 1, Dam 1d6, Mv 40', Sv F1, MI 12, XP 25 ea.

HP 7 ☐☐☐☐☐ ☐☐   7 ☐☐☐☐☐ ☐☐
    6 ☐☐☐☐☐ ☐   2 ☐☐

Skeletaire: AC 13, HD 1*, #At 1 dagger or spell, Dam 1d4 or per spell, Mv 40', Sv MU1, MI 12, XP 37

Spells: **darkness**

HP 4 ☐☐☐☐

Treasure: A **Scroll of Light and Charm Animal** is hidden in the fireplace.

5. FARIN'S CHAMBER:

> Farin's once splendid bedchamber is now a rotting space full of mold and mildew.

The two zombraires stand on either side of the door, waiting to attack. The yellow mold covers the fireplace and the floor immediately in front of the fireplace.

2 Zombraires: AC 12, HD 2*, #At 1 dagger or 1 spell, Dam 1d4 or per spell, Mv 40', Sv MU2, MI 9, XP 50 ea.

Spells: **sleep**

HP 4 ☐☐☐☐
   10 ☐☐☐☐☐ ☐☐☐☐☐

Yellow Mold: AC can always be hit, HD 2*, #At 1 spore burst, Dam 1d8/round for 6 rounds, Mv 0', Sv NM, MI 12, XP 100

HP 15 ☐☐☐☐☐ ☐☐☐☐☐ ☐☐☐☐☐

Treasure: A **Wand of Fireballs** with 8 uses remaining is in the fireplace.

6. STAIRS:

> The stairs extend down into the darkness below.

Any examination will show that the areas below are intended to be just as beautiful and vibrant as the areas above once were. However, they have also met a tarnished fate, although not quite as bad.

7. ACOLYTE'S DORMITORY:

> Crumbled beds and a few rotten priestly vestments are scattered about, as though they had been ransacked.

This was the male acolyte dormitory. The room has been searched by hungry ghouls hoping for a meal.

If the room is searched somewhat thoroughly, a **Ring of Protection +1** will be discovered lying under a small pile of rags.

8. ACOLYTE'S DORMITORY:

> The beds are broken and garments are strewn about wildly. This room has obviously been violently searched.

This room belonged to the female acolytes of Farin's temple. Like Area 7, this room has been searched by ghouls.

If the players search the room they will find a tattered and torn book that served at a diary. If the players read the diary, read the following.

> The pages are ripped and mostly missing, but what can be read says, "I have been growing worrisome of late. Father Farin believes himself... experiments and ghastly noises from deep. I fear that... holy master comments upon my youthfulness, and yet the noises and the stench... He is infallible, surely."
>
> The pages crumble upon being read.

9. CLASSROOM:

> Broken tables, chairs and parchment litter the room. Most things appear to have rotted and crumbled from years of age and neglect.

This was one of the rooms Farin and his priests used to teach locals before slowly indoctrinating them into Farin's personal faith. There is a small tithe box in the corner containing 5 gp, 27 sp, and 52 cp.

10. CLASSROOM:

> Broken tables, chairs and parchment litter the room. Most things appear to have rotted and crumbled from years of age and neglect.

This was another classroom used to bring in locals to Farin's faith. It more or less matches the classroom in Area 9.

If searched, this room contains a **Scroll of Charm Person and Ventriloquism**.

11. KITCHEN:

> A collection of pots and pans are scattered throughout.

The kitchen has become home to a family of giant rats (not the same ones from Area 2). These rats are eager to defend their territory and will attack at the first disturbance.

5 Giant Rats: AC 13, HD 1d4 hp, #At 1 bite, Dam 1d4 + disease, Mv 40', Sv F1, MI 8, XP 10 ea.

HP 4 ☐☐☐☐   2 ☐☐
    4 ☐☐☐☐   1 ☐
    3 ☐☐☐

12. STORAGE:

> The door to this room lies partially open. As you push the door open, a loud creaking can be heard, which startles the group of bats inside.

12 Bats: AC 14, HD 1 Hit Point, #At 1 special, Dam confusion, Mv 30', Fly 40', Sv NM, MI 6, XP 10 ea.

Each checkbox represents one bat

HP 12 ☐☐☐☐☐ ☐☐☐☐☐ ☐☐

13. PANTRY:

> The pantry contains a varied assortment of moldy grains and the rotted remains of what were once vegetables. The stench of rot and decay still remains.

The things that were once food are infested with rot grubs. Any disturbance of the area will also disturb the grubs and cause them to get on the characters.

14 Rot Grubs: AC 10, HD 1 Hit Point, #At 1 bite, Dam special, Mv 5', Sv F1, MI 12, XP 10 ea.

Each checkbox represents one rot grub

HP 14 ☐☐☐☐☐ ☐☐☐☐☐ ☐☐☐☐

14. AREA OF WORSHIP:

> The grand cathedral area of the temple seems to expand in all directions and still retains much of its grandness, despite the years of neglect. One column has fallen and broken to pieces.
>
> A dais raises slightly above the rest of the area. An altar upon the dais appears to be somewhat newer than the rest of the room and has an old book resting on it.

Hiding behind the rubble of the fallen column are a group of ghouls that have only recently started using this temple as a home. These are the creatures that locals have been using as part of their tales of ghosts.

3 Ghouls: AC 14, HD 2*, #At 2 claws/1 bite, Dam 1d4/1d4/1d4, all plus paralysis, Mv 30', Sv F2, Ml 9, XP 100 ea.

HP 10 ☐☐☐☐☐ ☐☐☐☐☐
   8 ☐☐☐☐☐ ☐☐☐
  11 ☐☐☐☐☐ ☐☐☐☐☐ ☐

Treasure: 27 gp, 3 iron spikes

If examined, the altar has a broken, wooden holy symbol resting on it next to the book. The book is old and difficult to read, but the characters can easily make out references to "powerful allies" and "sending forth the summons."

If the book is returned to the priesthood, they might be convinced to give the party 50 gp for preserving a piece of their history.

Middle Level Key

15. RUST MONSTER PEN:

> The sound of loud skittering and scratching can be heard even before the door is opened. Looking into the room reveals a pair of rust monsters excitedly pacing across the room.

The rust monsters take immediate notice of the characters. These creatures were used as guard animals by the cultists in hopes that anybody who would venture down into the depths would be turned back, or at the very least be disarmed.

Any metal thrown to the rust monsters will distract them from the player characters as they are quite hungry and a meal that doesn't fight back is always preferable.

2 Rust Monsters: AC 18, HD 5*, #At 1 antenna, Dam rust/corrosion destroys metal objects attacked, Mv 40', Sv F5, Ml 7, XP 405 ea.

HP 36 ☐☐☐☐☐ ☐☐☐☐☐ ☐☐☐☐☐ ☐☐☐☐☐
      ☐☐☐☐☐ ☐☐☐☐☐ ☐☐☐☐☐ ☐
  24 ☐☐☐☐☐ ☐☐☐☐☐ ☐☐☐☐☐ ☐☐☐☐☐
      ☐☐☐☐

16. SHADOW ROOM:

> As you enter the room, the door forcefully closes behind you. Any light you have with you seems to slightly dim from its once bright nature and a chill fills the air. It is then that you notice the dark shadows moving on their own.

The room is home to a group of shadows. When the door closes, it locks as if by a **wizard lock** cast by a 10th level magic-user, unlocking automatically only after all of the shadows are defeated.

In a small sack lying apparently discarded in a corner are 12 pp and a **Potion of Fire Resistance**; lying beside the sack is a **Cursed Mace -2**.

5 Shadows: AC 13‡, HD 2*, #At 1 touch, Dam 1d4 + 1 Strength loss, Mv 30', Sv F2, Ml 12, XP 100 ea.

HP 8 ☐☐☐☐☐ ☐☐☐
  12 ☐☐☐☐☐ ☐☐☐☐☐ ☐☐
   5 ☐☐☐☐☐
  11 ☐☐☐☐☐ ☐☐☐☐☐ ☐
   8 ☐☐☐☐☐ ☐☐☐

16A. ENTRANCE TO FARIN'S SECRET SANCTUARY:

> This closet area features a ladder that leads down. The bottom seems to just end abruptly without reason.

The entire floor of this closet is a hidden pit trap. A secret door at the bottom of the pit connects to room 21.

17. SECRET GARDEN:

> The room is filled with various herbs and mosses that can only be cultivated underground. The plants seem to draw moisture from some source below.

The room was clearly used to produce various plants to use in ceremonies and rituals, as well as possibly spices in meals. Five giant centipedes and a giant ghoul cockroach make this room their home.

The gate leading to the room from the hallway is locked. The trap door in the ceiling here is hidden (found as a secret door).

5 Giant Centipedes: AC 11, HD 1d4 hp*, #At 1 bite, Dam poison, Mv 40', Sv NM, MI 7, XP 13 ea.

HP 3 ☐☐☐ 4 ☐☐☐☐
2 ☐☐ 2 ☐☐
4 ☐☐☐☐

Giant Ghoul Cockroach: AC 16, HD 2**, #At 1 bite, Dam 1d6 + paralysis + disease, Mv 50', Sv F2, MI 12, XP 125

HP 12 ☐☐☐☐☐ ☐☐☐☐☐ ☐☐

18. EMPTY ROOM:

This room is barren of anything at all. It's very quiet in here. Almost too quiet.

If any character discovers the secret passage to Area 17, two wights will appear. They are two of Farin's former acolytes, cursed to haunt the room. If the characters arrive from Area 17, the wights will also appear.

The secret room connected to this area is a short corridor leading to an open 5' square pit. A set of iron rungs leads down 50' into the darkness, opening into a 10' cubical room with a trap door in the floor. It is this trap door that connects to room 17, above (which, perhaps somewhat confusingly, is below room 18).

2 Wights: AC 15†, HD 3*, #At 1 touch, Dam energy drain (1 level), Mv 30', Sv F3, MI 12, XP 175 ea.

HP 4 ☐☐☐☐ 4 ☐☐☐☐

19. HIDDEN STORAGE:

This appears to be a secret closet used by Farin before his death.

Farin, before he fully succumbed to his madness, grew paranoid, afraid that he might one day need to again take up arms against his enemies. He secreted his weapons and armor away, lest someone steal them. This closet contains a **Mace +3**, a suit of **Leather Armor +1**, and a **Potion of Invisibility**.

20. FARIN'S FINAL RESTING PLACE:

The room smells stale, as if no one has been in or out for quite some age. However, there are what appear to be a half-dozen lit torches all surrounding a stone crypt in the further recesses of the room. It is ornately carved and has a ring of bones surrounding it on the floor. The light of the torches brings out a strong red hue on the bones.

If the characters approach the crypt or attempt to leave the room without an interaction, Farin's ghostly form will appear above his grave. The spirit flies about the room, wailing and addressing the characters:

"I am dead, yet I can not die! Non-believers have defiled my resting place! Kill them, my followers!"

At his command, the bones around Farin's crypt will rise and attack the characters. Farin will vanish until the skeletons have been defeated, then he will reappear and attack the characters.

After defeating Farin's ghost, if the PCs examine his tomb they will find two **Potions of Healing**, a **Potion of Growth**, a **Scroll of Hold Person and Find Traps**, a **Scroll of 3 Magic-User Spells: Darkvision, Fireball, and Haste**, and a **Ring of Invisibility**.

The PCs will also find the book Farin preached from, which has been scrawled over in blood and used as a journal. The journal is quite valuable to the scholars associated with Farin's old faith, as well as many sages. It could easily fetch 900 gp from interested NPCs.

If the players read from the book, read or paraphrase the following text:

As you read the journal, it becomes quite clear that Farin had been manipulated into his delusions.

The journal reads, "I met with the scaled ones again today. I believe they are right. My divinity is all too clear now. I have merely had my eyes clouded by the world. Truly, if I keep bringing them what they ask for, I can return to my true form and my eternal life. Thankfully they remain below most times, though I still hear them sometimes in the night. Whatever work they perform, it is surely to glorify me. The chants and prayers are unfamiliar to my ears, but surely once my full divinity is restored to me..."

The journal entries afterward are nearly unreadable, rambling on in terms that can only be described as madness.

Farin had been influenced by a group of deep ones. One in particular, known as Vriruh, sought to corrupt a local faith into a cult and use it to commune with his own ancient gods. The results of such attempts lie below in the bottom level.

5 Crimson Bones Skeletons: AC 13, HD 2*,
#At 1 punch, Dam 1d6, Mv 50', Sv F2, Ml 12,
XP 100 ea.

HP 15 □□□□□ □□□□□ □□□□□
   6 □□□□□ □
   8 □□□□□ □□□
  13 □□□□□ □□□□□ □□□
   9 □□□□□ □□□□

Ghost of Farin: AC 20‡, HD 10*, #At 1 touch/1 gaze, Dam 1d8 + special, Mv 30', Sv F10, Ml 10, XP 1,390

HP 43 □□□□□ □□□□□ □□□□□ □□□□□
      □□□□□ □□□□□ □□□□□ □□□□□
      □□□

21. ANTECHAMBER:

Crude murals along the walls detail events of Farin's life, including preaching to the masses, building the temple, and so on. One strange image in particular features Farin holding a large fish in his hand with another resting on his head. Scattered about the room are various personal items as well as some clay jars.

The jars contain (in total) 258 gp, 122 sp, and 4 gems (worth 1,100 gp each). Most of the scattered items are worthless with the exception of a **Wand of Magic Detection**, a **Helm of Read Languages and Magic,** and a **Wand of Secret Door Detection**.

"Crypt of the Crimson Skeletons"

Lower Level Key

22. WELCOME TO THE THIRD FLOOR:

As you descend the stairs you notice the faint smell of rotting flesh mixed with an odor of fish.

The architecture here is similar to the other levels, though this one seems to have retained the ornateness intended. Age has still set in and some areas show decay and neglect, but this level still seems more revered than the previous two.

23. THE BATH:

Water drips from the ceiling and creeps in from the walls. It has formed small pools in the room roughly two feet deep, which have been cordoned off into individual tubs. The room is incredibly humid and cold.

The deep ones like to hydrate here, as well as use the area for rituals which connect them to their gods. There are three such deep ones here when the characters arrive. They are in deep meditation and do not initially notice the characters.

2 Common Deep Ones: AC 16, HD 3+3,
#At 2 claws, Dam 1d4/1d4, Mv 20' Swim 30', Sv F3,
MI 8, XP 145 ea.

HP 12 ☐☐☐☐☐ ☐☐☐☐☐ ☐☐
13 ☐☐☐☐☐ ☐☐☐☐☐ ☐☐☐

Hybrid Deep One: AC 14, HD 1+1, #At 2 claws,
Dam 1d2/1d2, Mv 30' Swim 20', Sv F1, MI 7, XP 25

HP 7 ☐☐☐☐☐ ☐☐

24. VRIRUH'S PERSONAL CHAMBERS:

It's dank and humid. The table at the back is covered with books, many obviously covered in mildew. The floor also seems littered with moldy scrolls and damp texts.

Vriruh has spent years upon years researching ancient and forbidden lore in hopes to know just the correct way to sway humans to do his bidding, as well as researching ways to have direct personal conversations with his gods.

The books and scrolls here could possibly be of interest to a sage or the local priesthood. Due to the shoddy nature of the items, they would not command an outstanding price (850 gp).

25. DINING OF THE DEEP ONES:

The room is a center of activity as a group of fish-like beings are busying themselves. They appear to be preparing meals, but one can only tell from the voracious looks on their faces.

These are some of the least of the deep ones here. As such they have been assigned to deal with meal preparation and other menial chores.

2 Common Deep Ones: AC 16, HD 3+3, #At 2 claws, Dam 1d4/1d4, Mv 20' Swim 30', Sv F3, MI 8, XP 145 ea.

HP 4 ☐☐☐☐   4 ☐☐☐☐

4 Hybrid Deep Ones: AC 14, HD 1+1, #At 2 claws, Dam 1d2/1d2, Mv 30' Swim 20', Sv F1, MI 7, XP 25 ea.

HP 1 ☐   1 ☐
1 ☐   1 ☐

26. DEEP WELL:

This room appears to be a well, dug deep into the earth. Water fills the well. Loud croaking can be heard quite easily.

The water in the well is pure and safe to drink. The deep ones consider their water a holy thing and try to keep it clean.

The croaking belongs to two giant frogs. The frogs will not initiate an attack but will retaliate if provoked.

2 Giant Frogs: AC 13, HD 2, #At 1 tongue or 1 bite, Dam grab or 1d4+1, Mv 30' Swim 30', Sv F2, MI 6, XP 75 ea.

HP 12 ☐☐☐☐☐ ☐☐☐☐☐ ☐☐
9 ☐☐☐☐☐ ☐☐☐☐

27. DANK AND MOLDY HALLWAY:

> The hallway stretches ahead for roughly 50 feet, but one can barely tell thanks to darkness that seems to permeate the area. The air is thick and humid, and breathing is difficult. The floor feels almost squishy beneath your feet.

Red Slime: AC 12, HD 2*, #At 1 slam, Dam 1d6 + 1d6 per round (and see below), Mv 10', Sv F2, Ml 12, XP 100

Note: On a successful attack the target is ensnared, and the victim suffers additional damage each round, applying damage inflicted to the slime's hit points. Each 6 points added above the normal hit point figure adds 1 hit die, to a maximum of 6 HD and 48 HP. Damage rises to 1d8 at 3 HD, 1d10 at 4 HD, 1d12 at 5 HD, and 2d8 at 6 HD.

HP   8   ☐☐☐☐☐ ☐☐☐

28. HALL AND FOYER:

> The hallway and area outside the doors found in the middle are all ornately decorated, far more than what would be expected of a floor this far below the surface. Ancient tapestries and crests line the walls.
>
> The two doors in the middle of the hallway are clearly masterwork creations and appear to depict what can only be surmised as dark gods and vile acts against humans and demihumans.

If the characters listen closely at the doors they can hear a faint sound like chanting coming from the other side. Though the doors appear heavy, they open quite easily.

29. ROOM OF THE DEEP ONES:

> This room appears to be some sort of living quarters for strange fishlike people. This is a very wet room with damp beds and other such furnishings.

There are three deep ones here. They appear to be preparing to return to their duties.

3 Common Deep Ones: AC 16, HD 3+3, #At 2 claws, Dam 1d4/1d4, Mv 20' Swim 30', Sv F3, Ml 8, XP 145 ea.

HP 20   ☐☐☐☐☐ ☐☐☐☐☐ ☐☐☐☐☐ ☐☐☐☐☐
     10   ☐☐☐☐☐ ☐☐☐☐☐
      8   ☐☐☐☐☐ ☐☐☐

30. DARK AREA:

> The floor appears to have a pool of thick, dark water spreading across it. Even stagnant water would not appear this thick. The slightest ripple catches your eyes and it is at this moment that you realize, the dark form is moving toward you.

The hallway leading here is clearly a more recent addition to the area than the rest, though not new by any standard of time.

A black pudding has made its way into this room from the underground recesses beneath the temple's lower floors, especially given the shoddy construction of this room. It is hungry and eager for a meal. It will fight to the death.

Black Pudding*: AC 14, HD 10*, AB +9, #At 1 pseudopod, Dam 3d8, Mv 20', Sv F10, Ml 12, XP 1,390

Note: If attacked with weapons or lightning the pudding takes no damage but is split in two, dividing hit points and hit dice between them, to a minimum of 2 HD. Hit point boxes below have been divided up into four groups for 3, 2, 3, and 2 HD versions respectively (as a 10 HD monster divided the maximum number of times would result in those figures). The GM should distribute damage inflicted (which does not split the monster) between the groups roughly equally.

HP 26   ☐☐☐☐☐ ☐☐   ☐☐☐☐☐ ☐
         ☐☐☐☐☐ ☐☐   ☐☐☐☐☐ ☐

31. PRISON:

> Several sets of shackles are attached to the wall, indicating this was once an area used to keep prisoners, possibly for sacrifice. It is currently empty and seems to have been for quite some time.

This area contains no monsters, treasure, or traps.

32. ROOM OF PUNISHMENT:

> This room is lined with items used for torture. A wooden slab in the back of the room is clearly used to chain down offenders while they are flogged.

None of the torture implements are of any use to the players. Thankfully, there is no one currently present in this room.

33. GRAND HALL:

> The room opens with descending stairs that lead to a grand open room that appears to be the perfected form of the worship area in the main temple. Along the walls are treasure chests that appear to be leftover from Farin's old congregation.
>
> Amid the columns is a large fish-like humanoid creature. It can be heard chanting in a guttural language. It takes little notice of you, and signals to other creatures who have been secluded among the columns.

The chanting creature is Vriruh, the sorcerer-priest of this group of deep ones. He is the one who corrupted Farin to begin with, and he is in the process of trying to contact his gods. This attempt will actually result in summoning a tentacled horror from a different plane.

The deep ones Vriruh motioned to will not flee from the battle.

4 Common Deep Ones: AC 16, HD 3+3, #At 2 claws, Dam 1d4/1d4, Mv 20' Swim 30', Sv F3, Ml 12, XP 145 ea.

HP   8 ☐☐☐☐☐ ☐☐☐
     15 ☐☐☐☐☐ ☐☐☐☐☐ ☐☐☐☐☐
     16 ☐☐☐☐☐ ☐☐☐☐☐ ☐☐☐☐☐ ☐
     16 ☐☐☐☐☐ ☐☐☐☐☐ ☐☐☐☐☐ ☐

2 Hybrid Deep Ones: AC 14, HD 1+1, #At 2 claws, Dam 1d2/1d2, Mv 30' Swim 20', Sv F1, Ml 12, XP 25 ea.

HP   5 ☐☐☐☐☐   2 ☐☐

If Vriruh is not interrupted for at least 4 rounds, a tentacled horror will appear and both will then attack the party in full force. However, Vriruh will also take any opportunity to escape. If he manages to make it out of the room, consider him to have escaped to work his evil elsewhere.

> As the last of the deep one guards lie at your feet, you notice that Vriruh has finished his ritual. Whatever he may have been attempting, the results are now quite obvious. A mass of writhing tentacles now sits upon the dais.
>
> Vriruh attempts to address the characters in the common tongue. "Not... gods intended. Still... slay infidels!"

Vriruh, Deep One Sorcerer-priest: AC 17, HD 8, #At 2 claws, Dam 1d4/1d4, Mv 30' Swim 30', Sv F6, Ml 10, XP 675

Spells: **darkness, cause fear, resist fire, cause disease, animate dead, create water**

HP 30 ☐☐☐☐☐ ☐☐☐☐☐ ☐☐☐☐☐ ☐☐☐☐☐
         ☐☐☐☐☐ ☐☐☐☐☐

Tentacled Horror: AC 14, HD 10+20*, #At 5 tentacles + crush, Dam 1d6 tentacle, 3d6 crush, Mv 30', Sv F10, Ml 12, XP 1,390

HP 52 ☐☐☐☐☐ ☐☐☐☐☐ ☐☐☐☐☐ ☐☐☐☐☐
         ☐☐☐☐☐ ☐☐☐☐☐ ☐☐☐☐☐ ☐☐☐☐☐
         ☐☐☐☐☐ ☐☐☐☐☐ ☐☐

There are four treasure chests in the room. Contained within are 12 silver short bow arrows, a **Cloak of Displacement**, a **Ring of Fire Resistance**, a **Longsword +1, +3 vs. lycanthropes, casts light on command**, 1 **Potion of Control Animal**, 1 **Potion of Heroism**, and 10 gems (total value 6,000 gp).

Descent Into Culwich
by James Lemon

Setting the Mood

Whether it's day or night, there's a storm coming when the players approach the temple. The sea air is picking up, thunder booms in the distance, and a few splotches of rain can be felt.

Wandering Monsters

The GM should roll for a random encounter each turn the adventurers are in a corridor, and every other turn when they are not. Roll 1d6; on a 1, one of the following encounters will occur.

1. **2 Shriekers:** AC 13, HD 3, #At Special, Dam None, Mv 5', Sv F1, MI 12, XP 145 ea.
   HP   9   □□□□□ □□□□
        13   □□□□□ □□□□□ □□□

2. **Black Pudding:** AC 14, HD 10* (+9), #At 1 pseudopod, Dam 3d8, Mv 20', Sv F10, MI 12, XP 1,390
   Note: If attacked with weapons or lightning the pudding takes no damage but is split in two, dividing hit points and hit dice between them, to a minimum of 2 HD. Hit point boxes below have been divided up into four groups for 3, 2, 3, and 2 HD versions respectively (as a 10 HD monster divided the maximum number of times would result in those figures). The GM should distribute damage inflicted (which does not split the monster) between the groups roughly equally.
   HP   43   □□□□□ □□□□□ □□□
             □□□□□ □□□□
             □□□□□ □□□□□ □□□
             □□□□□ □□□

3. **3 Blink Dogs:** AC 15, HD 4*, #At 1 bite, Dam 1d6, Mv 40', Sv F4, MI 6, XP 280 ea.
   HP   19   □□□□□ □□□□□ □□□□□
             □□□□
        15   □□□□□ □□□□□ □□□□□
        13   □□□□□ □□□□□ □□□

4. **6 Giant Centipedes:** AC 11, HD 1d4 HP*, #At 1 bite, Dam poison, Mv 40', Sv NM, MI 7, XP 13 ea.
   HP   4   □□□□   3   □□□
        2   □□   4   □□□□
        3   □□□   2   □□

5. **3 Dopplegangers:** AC 15, HD 4*, #At 1 fist, Dam 1d12 or by weapon, Mv 30', Sv F4, MI 10, XP 280 ea.
   HP   19   □□□□□ □□□□□ □□□□□
             □□□□
        13   □□□□□ □□□□□ □□□
        15   □□□□□ □□□□□ □□□□□

6. **Gelatinous Cube:** AC 12, HD 4*, #At 1, Dam 2d4+paralysis, Mv 20', Sv F2, MI 12, XP 280
   HP   20   □□□□□ □□□□□ □□□□□
             □□□□□

Upper Level Key

1. PORTICO:

As you approach the temple you see a raised platform with pillars on each side of the central doors, wrapping around the corner. Most are crumbling, but still stand at least ten feet tall. On the left and right of the raised platform are several rose bushes, growing to the corners of the temple. There are two large green orbs implanted into the wall on either side behind the pillars.

The green orbs are high off the ground, and are immune to physical damage. The double doors aren't locked, but it will take at least two higher-strength characters to get them open. The rose bushes are actually blood roses; if the players stay on the platform they won't react, but if they step off the platform near the roses they will have a 1 in 1d6 chance of smelling its scent on the sea air.

6 Blood Roses: AC 13, HD 3*, #At 1 to 3 + blood drain, Dam 1d6, Mv 1', Sv F2, MI 12, XP 175 ea.
HP   17   □□□□□ □□□□□ □□□□□ □□
     12   □□□□□ □□□□□ □□
     20   □□□□□ □□□□□ □□□□□ □□□□□
      9   □□□□□ □□□□
     12   □□□□□ □□□□□ □□
      9   □□□□□ □□□□

2. FOYER:

As soon as you open the doors you notice the holes in the roof above, lending to the cooler-than-expected air in here. Straight ahead are another set of double doors, and to the left and right are single doors. There is a large hanging light fixture, with three large orbs emanating yellow light. Ahead of the doors, on the left and right walls, are large paintings depicting men and women gathered in the countryside.

There is nothing of interest in this area.

3. LARGE BEDROOM:

The roof in here is mostly intact, but it doesn't insulate from the increasing thunder outside. There is a heavy layer of dust over the chairs and table in the middle. There is a large fireplace opposite the door on the west wall; it is oddly empty and clean. On the east side is a heavy and intricate mass of webbing, growing out up to the ceiling. There are skeletons of rats and other small creatures on the floor and stuck into the web. Even in torchlight you can barely see two large black masses in the corners.

2 Giant Black Widow Spiders: AC 14, HD 3*, #At 1 bite, Dam 2d6+poison, Mv 20' Web 40', Sv F3, MI 8, XP 175 ea.

HP 9 □□□□□ □□□□
    8 □□□□□ □□□

4. PARLOR:

Upon opening the door you see several large holes in the roof. On the opposite wall is a large fireplace, filled with soaked logs and ash. In the northwest and southwest corner three bats are hanging from the ceiling, asleep.

Unless the PCs make loud noises the giant bats won't awaken (due to the noises from the storm).

3 Giant Bats: AC 14, HD 2, #At 1 bite, Dam 1d4, Mv 10' Fly 60' (10'), Sv F2, MI 8, XP 75 ea.

HP 8 □□□□□ □□□
    7 □□□□□ □□
   10 □□□□□ □□□□□

5. LARGE BEDROOM:

The roof in here is completely intact, lending to much drier air. Opposite the door is a small fireplace with several logs in it.

If the PCs light the logs on fire, it will illuminate a scrawled message on the southeast wall: "Beware the black mist". This message can't be viewed with any other light.

6. STAIRWELL:

Ahead are stairs leading down; they are quite steep, and require a hand on the wall to steady oneself. After a few flights the stairs bend left, and you come to a landing, with one more flight of stairs down. In front of you is a large door, and to the left are another set of straight stairs further down.

The door to access the stairs is locked, and requires the key from area 13.

7. NARROW ROOM:

Several large holes in the roof have given way to a large puddle/pond of mucky water in the southwest corner. You hear a sloshing sound.

Giant Leech: AC 17, HD 6, #At 1 bite+hold, Dam 1d6+1d6/round, Mv 30', Sv F6, MI 10, XP 500

HP 26 □□□□□ □□□□□ □□□□□ □□□□□
       □□□□□ □

8. STOREROOM:

There are several smaller holes in the roof, but it looks like someone patched them. On the east and north walls are floor-to-ceiling shelving, filled with barrels, bottles, and jugs of various drink.

If the PCs smell or taste any of the stored drinks they will discover various ales, meads, wines, and ports; all are still fresh.

9. STOREROOM:

The roof is intact in here. There are large piles of hay and sacks of dry food stores stacked against the west wall.

If the PCs disturb anything, the giant rats will emerge and attack.

4 Giant Rats: AC 13, HD 1d4HP, #At 1 bite,
Dam 1d4+disease, Mv 40' Swim 20', Sv F1, MI 8,
XP 10 ea.

HP   1 ☐   4 ☐☐☐☐
      2 ☐☐   3 ☐☐☐

10. ROOM OF THE DEAD:

> As soon as you open the door you see corpses piled everywhere. Even at a cursory glance you see various races including human, orc, and more.

If the PCs disturb any of the bodies they risk the rot grubs attaching and penetrating their skin.

5 Rot Grubs: AC 10, HD 1 HP, #At 1 bite,
Dam special, Mv 5', Sv F1, MI 12, XP 10 ea.

Each checkbox represents one rot grub

HP   5 ☐☐☐☐☐

11. PANTRY:

> As soon as you open the door you can smell the cured and smoked meats and cheeses. They are piled up on shelves, as well as hanging from the ceiling. Even at a cursory glance you can tell many have been opened and nibbled on.

4 Giant Rats: AC 13, HD 1d4 HP, #At 1 bite,
Dam 1d4+disease, Mv 40' Swim 20', Sv F1, MI 8,
XP 10 ea.

HP   1 ☐   4 ☐☐☐☐
      2 ☐☐   3 ☐☐☐

12. DORMITORY:

> There are makeshift beds lined up against the walls. Old worn shoes and clothes are piled onto and beside each one.

There is nothing of interest in this room.

13. OFFICE:

> Against the opposite wall is a very large, wide desk, with a set of four drawers on each side. On top is a writing quill in its holder, three bottles of ink of different colors, and several sheets of papyrus with indecipherable scribblings on each one.

The key to area 6 is located in the middle right drawer. All but two drawers are locked, and to open them they must be fully pulled out in a certain order, with the final drawer being the one with the key. This pattern is left up to the GM to decide.

14. SANCTUARY:

> Upon opening the doors you notice that almost the entire roof is gone! There is a row of pillars on each side parallel to the walls. Similar to the ones out front these are in various states of decay, but the back left pillar has completely collapsed. The air is even cooler in here, the humidity from the nearby sea soaked into everything.
>
> Walking past the rows of rotting wooden pews, the walls flare out for about twenty feet before turning to meet each other at the back of the sanctuary. The back half of this large open area is a raised dais, with a surprisingly small altar in the center. The left-side wall behind the dais has a large hole in it. Stone fragments and other debris litter the dais.

Astute PCs will observe that all of the debris is inside, and not outside... Lined on each side of the altar parallel to the back walls are six gargoyles, each perched on a large obsidian base in different poses. They will not attack unless a PC moves within two feet.

6 Gargoyles: AC 15‡, HD 4**, #At 2 claws/1 bite/1 horn, Dam 1d4/1d4/1d6/1d4, Mv 30' Fly 50' (15'), Sv F6, MI 11, XP 320 ea.

HP   14 ☐☐☐☐☐ ☐☐☐☐☐ ☐☐☐☐
     19 ☐☐☐☐☐ ☐☐☐☐☐ ☐☐☐☐☐ ☐☐☐☐
     25 ☐☐☐☐☐ ☐☐☐☐☐ ☐☐☐☐☐ ☐☐☐☐☐
         ☐☐☐☐☐
     16 ☐☐☐☐☐ ☐☐☐☐☐ ☐☐☐☐☐ ☐
     12 ☐☐☐☐☐ ☐☐☐☐☐ ☐☐
     15 ☐☐☐☐☐ ☐☐☐☐☐ ☐☐☐☐☐

Behind the altar are several leather sacks, containing 2,000 cp, 600 ep, and 1 statuette (worth 700 gp).

Middle Level Key

15. MOLDY ROOM:

> You notice the door is extremely moldy, slime reflecting any torch or other light. Forcing the door open, you see patches of mold and mildew all over the walls and ceiling.

While most of the mold and mildew is fairly benign unless the PCs disturb it or stay in the room too long, on the back wall is a distinct patch of yellow mold.

Yellow Mold: AC can always be hit, HD 2*, #At 1 spore burst, Dam 1d8/round for 6 rounds, Mv 0', Sv NM, Ml 12, XP 100

HP   7   ☐☐☐☐☐ ☐☐

16. RATTY DORMITORY:

> There are several small beds against the north and south walls, and a table near the door on the west wall. Sitting around it are four small humanoids with twitchy noses and mouth, and small black beady eyes.

4 Lycanthrope, Wererats: AC 13†, HD 3*, #At 1 bite or 1 weapon, Dam 1d4 or 1d6 or by weapon, Mv 40', Sv F3, Ml 8, XP 175 ea.

HP   9   ☐☐☐☐☐ ☐☐☐☐
       13   ☐☐☐☐☐ ☐☐☐☐☐ ☐☐☐
       13   ☐☐☐☐☐ ☐☐☐☐☐ ☐☐☐
       16   ☐☐☐☐☐ ☐☐☐☐☐ ☐☐☐☐☐ ☐

Tucked under the beds is 1,800 cp, 1,500 sp, and 600 ep.

16A. TRAP ROOM:

The door is locked; the key is on one of the wererat's person.

The entire floor of this closet is a hidden pit trap. A secret door at the bottom of the pit connects to room 21.

17. BODY DUMP:

> There is a pile of skeletons in the northwest corner. Weapons, shields, and other items are scattered across the room. In the southeast corner is a gate of wrought iron.

The trap door in the ceiling here is hidden (found as a secret door). Scrounging around in one of the piles of weapons and armor is a rust monster.

Rust Monster: AC 18, HD 5*, #At 1 antenna, Dam rust/corrosion destroys metal objects attacked, Mv 40', Sv F5, Ml 7, XP 405

HP   19   ☐☐☐☐☐ ☐☐☐☐☐ ☐☐☐☐☐ ☐☐☐☐

If the players take the time to search through all the items and the pile of skeletons, they will find in total 2,400 gp, 2,800 sp, a pearl (worth 500 gp), a topaz (worth 500 gp), a sardonyx (worth 50 gp), a **Potion of Fire Resistance**, a **Scroll of Protection from Evil**, and a **Scroll of Protection from Lycanthropes**.

18. SHADOWY ROOM:

> There are large yellow orbs embedded in the walls, flickering light at random. Every time one of them does, you swear there was something else in the room with you.

The secret room connected to this area is a short corridor leading to an open 5' square pit. A set of iron rungs leads down 40' into the darkness, opening into a 10' cubical room with a trap door in the floor. It is this trap door that connects to room 17, above (which, perhaps somewhat confusingly, is below room 18).

2 Shadows: AC 13‡, HD 2*, #At 1 touch, Dam 1d4 + 1 point Strength loss, Mv 30', Sv F2, Ml 12, XP 100 ea.

HP   11   ☐☐☐☐☐ ☐☐☐☐☐ ☐
        8   ☐☐☐☐☐ ☐☐☐

Piled in the northeast corner are 1,800 gp, 1,000 pp, 1 **Potion of Healing**, 1 **Scroll of Protection from Lycanthropes**, 1 **Scroll of Protection from Magic**, and 1 **Scroll of Three Magic-User Spells** (**continual darkness, ESP, protection from normal missiles**).

19. SECRET ROOM:

> There is a large wooden chest of drawers against the wall, and two large green crystal orbs inset in the ceiling, casting a soft green light.

Inside the chest of drawers is 4,800 gp, 1,100 pp, 1 **Map to Type G Treasure** (far from the temple), 1 **Potion of Heroism**, and 1 **Ring of Fire Resistance**.

20. WORMHOLES:

> The floor in this room is bare dirt, mounded anywhere from several inches to a foot or more in some areas. There are several large holes in the right-hand wall, some filled in with dirt while others are partially open.

If the PCs spend more than 1 round in the room, the tentacle worms will emerge from the holes in the wall.

2 Tentacle Worms: AC 13, HD 3*, #At 6 tentacles, Dam paralysis, Mv 40', Sv F3, Ml 9, XP 175 ea.

HP 13 ☐☐☐☐☐ ☐☐☐☐☐ ☐☐☐
   20 ☐☐☐☐☐ ☐☐☐☐☐ ☐☐☐☐☐ ☐☐☐☐☐

If the PCs take the time to sift through all the dirt on the floor, they will find 2,100 cp, 1,100 ep, 1,300 gp, a jeweled golden brooch (worth 900 gp), and a braided platinum chain (worth 1,300 gp).

21. DISPLACER LAIR:

> As soon as you open the door you see several large cats; as you look at them, they seems to move around, yet their feet remain planted on the floor. Then long tentacles edged with what look like sharp teeth rise up from their shoulders, almost like wings, and wave menacingly at you.

3 Displacers: AC 16, HD 6*, #At 2 blades, Dam 1d8/1d8, Mv 50', Sv F6, Ml 8, XP 555 ea.

HP 24 ☐☐☐☐☐ ☐☐☐☐☐ ☐☐☐☐☐ ☐☐☐☐☐
      ☐☐☐☐
   26 ☐☐☐☐☐ ☐☐☐☐☐ ☐☐☐☐☐ ☐☐☐☐☐
      ☐☐☐☐☐ ☐
   31 ☐☐☐☐☐ ☐☐☐☐☐ ☐☐☐☐☐ ☐☐☐☐☐
      ☐☐☐☐☐ ☐☐☐☐☐ ☐

Taking the time to search through all the rubble and mess will yield 2,000 gp, 1 pearl (worth 500 gp), 2 peridots (worth 100 gp each), a **Potion of Polymorph Self**, and a **Scroll of Protection from Elementals**.

Lower Level Key

22. ENTRY:

> Across the room there is another door in the west wall, boarded up so completely that you can barely see the door itself. Piled in front of the other door are piles of barrels shored up with sandbags. On the north wall next to the door is an arrow pointing at it, drawn in what appears to be blood.

Other than the things described above, there is nothing of interest in this room. The barrels all contained brackish (salty) water, but some leaked out long ago.

23. ZOMBIES:

> There are four beds against the walls, each with a rotting corpse on it. Suddenly they sit up and groan in unison.

4 Zombies: AC 12, HD 2, #At 1 weapon, Dam 1d8 or by weapon, Mv 20', Sv F2, Ml 12, XP 75 ea.

HP 10 ☐☐☐☐☐ ☐☐☐☐☐
   15 ☐☐☐☐☐ ☐☐☐☐☐ ☐☐☐☐☐
   13 ☐☐☐☐☐ ☐☐☐☐☐ ☐☐☐
   10 ☐☐☐☐☐ ☐☐☐☐☐

24. CLOSET:

> There are shelves lining the walls, filled with tattered clothing, bedding, and cleaning supplies.

There is nothing of interest in this room.

25. OFFICE:

> There are several large desks against the walls, each made from a different wood. Each has various books and writing materials on it. There is a large round inset medallion in the northwest corner, and next to it is a small hole.

None of the desks have anything in their drawers. The medallion cannot be removed, and if pressed it sinks in for a few seconds before returning flush to the wall. It must be pressed at the same time as the one in area 26 to open the secret stone panels. The hole is about an inch wide, but there is no easy way to determine where it ends. Anyone speaking into the hole can be heard in area 26, so that two PCs can press the medallions simultaneously.

26. BATH:

> There are small orbs embedded into the walls, emanating soft light that slowly shifts through the color spectrum. There are two large empty tubs, each with a wood sidetable with soaps and brushes on them. Beside them are empty wooden buckets. There is a large round inset medallion in the south wall, and next to it is a small hole.

The medallion cannot be removed, and if pressed it sinks in for a few seconds before returning flush to the wall. It must be pressed at the same time as the one in area 25 for the secret stone panels to open. The hole is the other end of the narrow opening connecting to the hole in area 25.

27. WRAITHS:

> You can see a single source of light shining from the inset wall in the middle of the north side. Within the soft glow in this hallway you see shifting humanoid shapes.

2 Wraiths: AC 15‡, HD 4**, #At 1 touch, Dam 1d6 + energy drain (1 level), Mv Fly 80', Sv F4, MI 12, XP 320 ea.

HP 27 □□□□□ □□□□□ □□□□□ □□□□□ □□□□□ □□
25 □□□□□ □□□□□ □□□□□ □□□□□ □□□□□

On the ground below the embedded yellow orb are 2,200 gp, 600 cp, 1 **Bag of Holding**, 1 **Cursed Scroll**, and 1 **Potion of Delusion**.

28. STATUE GALLERY:

> Coming around the corner, you see two doors side-by-side in the middle of the north wall, with two large metal statues on each side. Opposite the doors, the wall is set back ten feet. Within that additional space is a shallow, wide table, covered in a mass of candles now all melted into one gigantic waxy blob, with only a few stray wicks sticking up. Above the table is a framed painting of an old man in robes. At the other end of the hall it turns left, ending at a door.

At the west end of the hall is a secret door.

4 Iron Living Statues: AC 18, HD 4*, #At 2 fists, Dam 1d8/1d8+special, Mv 10', Sv F4, MI 12, XP 280 ea.

HP 15 □□□□□ □□□□□ □□□□□
17 □□□□□ □□□□□ □□□□□ □□
16 □□□□□ □□□□□ □□□□□ □
17 □□□□□ □□□□□ □□□□□ □□

29. OOZE:

> Stacked against the south wall is a row of barrels. In front of it are piles of broken barrels, chairs, and other furniture.

If any of the PCs disturb the pile near the back, the gray ooze will emerge and attack.

Gray Ooze: AC 12, HD 3*, #At 1 pseudopod, Dam 2d8, Mv 1', Sv F3, MI 12, XP 175

HP 17 □□□□□ □□□□□ □□□□□ □□

30. SPECTRE:

> At the end of this long hallway you see a door slightly ajar, with wavering blue light pulsating through the open space. Pushing the door open enough to peek around, you see a floating hexagonal blue gem in the northeast corner, rotating and shining blue light with every turn. Sitting in the northeast corner in a plush chair is a man in robes, with a large slashing wound across his chest.

This light is harmless, but if anyone touches the gem with bare hands they will receive 1d6 points of frost damage per turn/round.

Spectre*: AC 17‡, HD 6**, #At 1 touch, Dam energy drain 2 lvls/touch, Mv Fly 100', Sv F6, MI 11, XP 610

HP 32 □□□□□ □□□□□ □□□□□ □□□□□ □□□□□ □□□□□ □□

Piled on both sides of the chair are 1,100 ep, 1 **Potion of Gaseous Form**, 1 **Scroll of Darkvision**, 1 **Scroll of Six Magic-User Spells (anti-magic shell, clairvoyance, continual light, dispel magic, knock, wizard eye)**, and a **Shield +1**.

31. ARMORY:

> Against the north wall is a rack of weapons, containing various swords, axes, and a couple maces, hammers, and longbows. Opposite the door is a stand with a suit of plate mail armor. Hanging on the south wall are two shields.

None of the weapons listed are magical. If anyone wishes to look for a specific weapon, the GM should decide whether or not the weapon is present.

Other than the items listed, there is nothing of interest in this room.

32. BEDROOM:

> In the southwest corner is a bed, flanked by lit torches on either side. Lying on the bed is a young woman in a white dress.

The young woman is in fact a medusa. Note that any surprised individuals will probably meet her gaze automatically, unless she is also surprised. A saving throw still applies, of course.

Medusa: AC 12, HD 4**, #At 1 snakebite+gaze, Dam 1d6+poison+petrification, Mv 30', Sv F4, MI 8, XP 320

HP 15 ☐☐☐☐☐ ☐☐☐☐☐ ☐☐☐☐☐

Underneath the bed are 900 pp, 1 **Potion of Clairvoyance**, 1 **Scroll of Protection from Undead**, and 1 **Scroll of Three Clerical Spells (remove fear*, silence 15' radius, speak with dead)**.

33. FIEND'S LAIR:

> A small landing sits above two flights of stairs going down. You can see the bottom of the stairs are illuminated in bright red light. As you reach the bottom of the stairs you find yourself standing on a raised dais. Embedded in the east and west walls are large red orbs about ten feet up, spaced out every twenty feet. There are four large pillars on each side parallel to the walls, the first of which are set into the dais.

> Crouched at the north end against the curved wall is a large humanoid figure, rising to its feet. Large spiraled horns and tucked wings are the first thing you notice, then you notice where its legs should be is fading black smoke.

Note: For details on the Shadow Fiend, see the **Basic Fantasy Field Guide Volume 2**.

Shadow Fiend (Infernal): AC 18‡, HD 8*, #At 1 touch or 1 spell, Dam 1d6, Mv Fly 180', Sv T14, MI 9, XP 665

HP 46 ☐☐☐☐☐ ☐☐☐☐☐ ☐☐☐☐☐ ☐☐☐☐☐
       ☐☐☐☐☐ ☐☐☐☐☐ ☐☐☐☐☐ ☐☐☐☐☐
       ☐☐☐☐☐ ☐

Piled behind the northeast pillar are 1,500 gp, 1 **Ring of Protection + 1**, 1 **Scroll of Protection from Elementals**, and 1 **Shortbow + 3**.

Upper Level Map

All maps are scaled at 1 square = 10 feet.

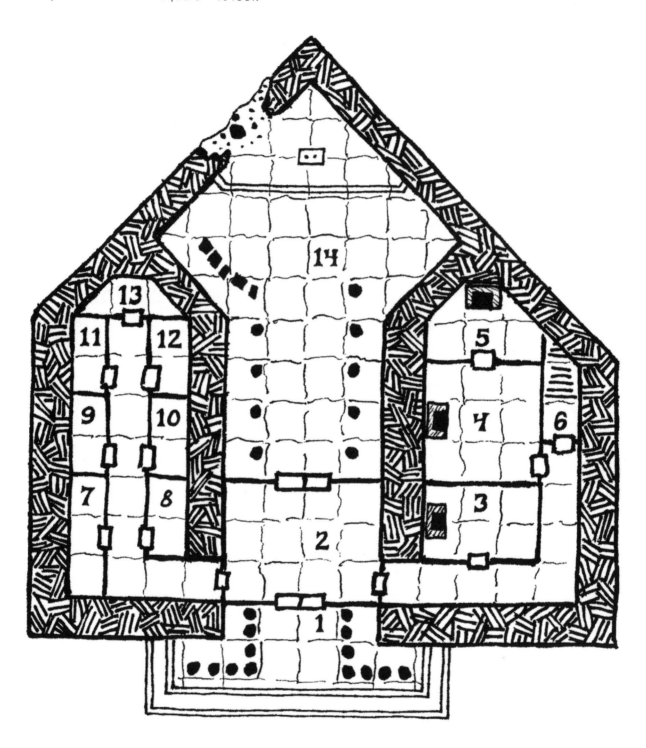

Middle Level Map

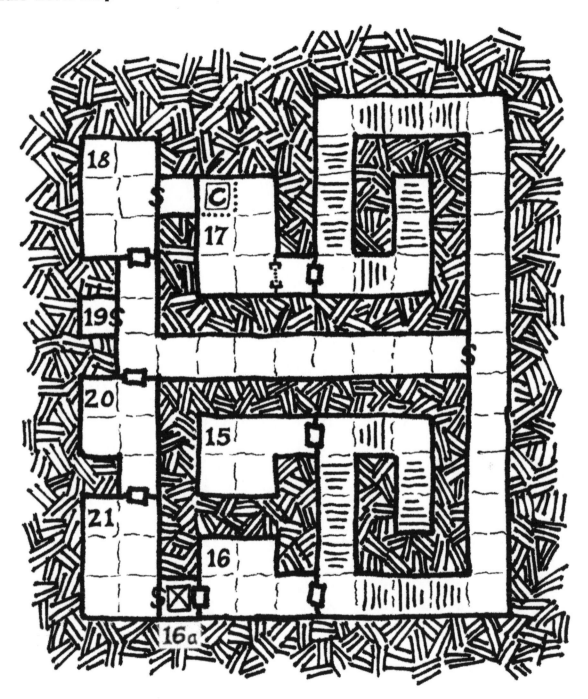

Middle Level, Rooms 17-18 Detail

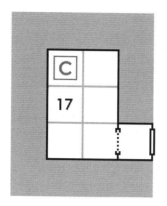

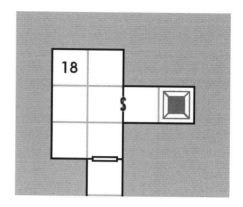

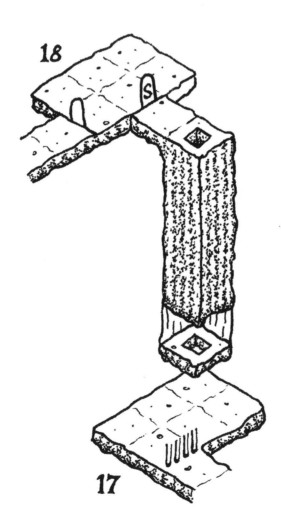

Middle Level, 3D View

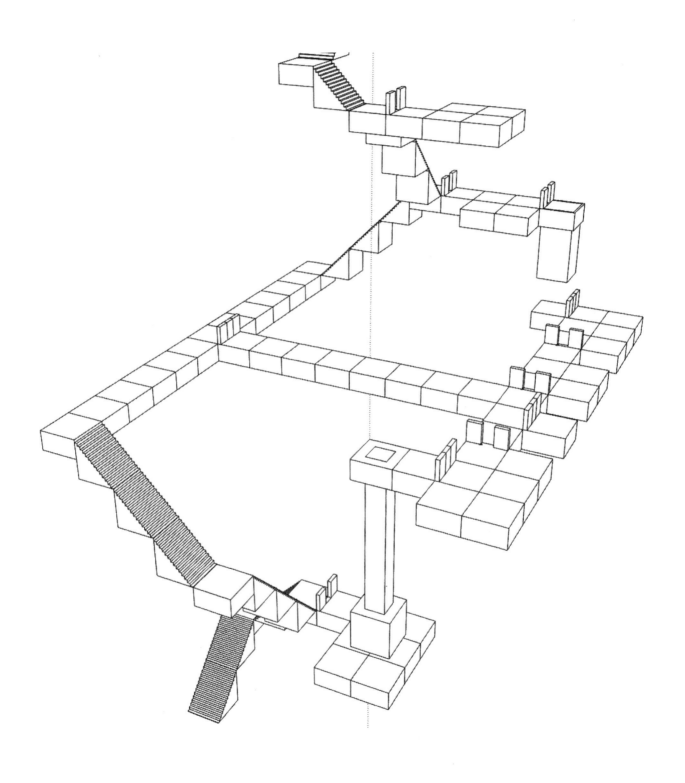

Lower Level

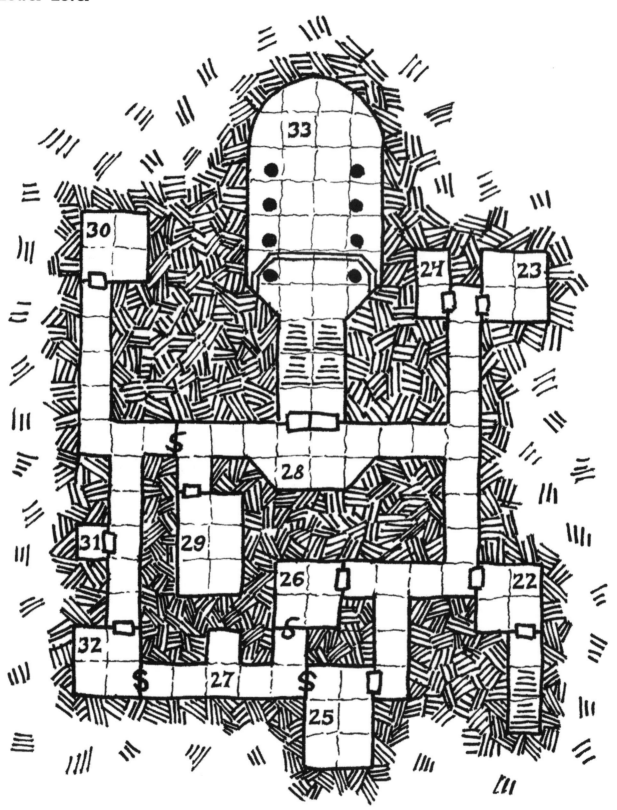

Open Game License

Designation of Open Game Content: The entire text of **The Dark Temple** (except the Open Game License, as explained below) is Open Game Content, released under the Open Game License, Version 1.0a (reproduced below) as described in Section 1(d) of the License. Artwork incorporated in this document is not Open Game Content, and remains the property of the copyright holder.

Designation of Product Identity: Product identity is not Open Game Content. The following is designated as product identity pursuant to OGL v1.0a(1)(e) and (7): (A) product and product line names, including Basic Fantasy Role-Playing Game; (B) all artwork, logos, symbols, graphic designs, depictions, likenesses, formats, poses, concepts, themes and graphic, photographic and other visual representations, including the "eye" logo, which is the personal trademark of Chris Gonnerman for his various products; (C) logos and trademarks, including any trademark or registered trademark clearly identified as product identity by the owner of the product identity, and which specifically excludes the open game content.

More information on the Open Game License can be found at:

http://www.wizards.com/d20

The terms of the Open Game License Version 1.0a are as follows:

The following text is the property of Wizards of the Coast, Inc. and is Copyright 2000 Wizards of the Coast, Inc ("Wizards"). All Rights Reserved.

1. Definitions: (a)"Contributors" means the copyright and/or trademark owners who have contributed Open Game Content; (b)"Derivative Material" means copyrighted material including derivative works and translations (including into other computer languages), potation, modification, correction, addition, extension, upgrade, improvement, compilation, abridgment or other form in which an existing work may be recast, transformed or adapted; (c) "Distribute" means to reproduce, license, rent, lease, sell, broadcast, publicly display, transmit or otherwise distribute; (d)"Open Game Content" means the game mechanic and includes the methods, procedures, processes and routines to the extent such content does not embody the Product Identity and is an enhancement over the prior art and any additional content clearly identified as Open Game Content by the Contributor, and means any work covered by this License, including translations and derivative works under copyright law, but specifically excludes Product Identity. (e) "Product Identity" means product and product line names, logos and identifying marks including trade dress; artifacts; creatures characters; stories, storylines, plots, thematic elements, dialogue, incidents, language, artwork, symbols, designs, depictions, likenesses, formats, poses, concepts, themes and graphic, photographic and other visual or audio representations; names and descriptions of characters, spells, enchantments, personalities, teams, personas, likenesses and special abilities; places, locations, environments, creatures, equipment, magical or supernatural abilities or effects, logos, symbols, or graphic designs; and any other trademark or registered trademark clearly identified as Product identity by the owner of the Product Identity, and which specifically excludes the Open Game Content; (f) "Trademark" means the logos, names, mark, sign, motto, designs that are used by a Contributor to identify itself or its products or the associated products contributed to the Open Game License by the Contributor (g) "Use", "Used" or "Using" means to use, Distribute, copy, edit, format, modify, translate and otherwise create Derivative Material of Open Game Content. (h) "You" or "Your" means the licensee in terms of this agreement.

2. The License: This License applies to any Open Game Content that contains a notice indicating that the Open Game Content may only be Used under and in terms of this License. You must affix such a notice to any Open Game Content that you Use. No terms may be added to or subtracted from this License except as described by the License itself. No other terms or conditions may be applied to any Open Game Content distributed using this License.

3.Offer and Acceptance: By Using the Open Game Content You indicate Your acceptance of the terms of this License.

4. Grant and Consideration: In consideration for agreeing to use this License, the Contributors grant You a perpetual, worldwide, royalty-free, non-exclusive license with the exact terms of this License to Use, the Open Game Content.

5.Representation of Authority to Contribute: If You are contributing original material as Open Game Content, You represent that Your Contributions are Your original creation and/or You have sufficient rights to grant the rights conveyed by this License.

6.Notice of License Copyright: You must update the COPYRIGHT NOTICE portion of this License to include the exact text of the COPYRIGHT NOTICE of any Open Game Content You are copying, modifying or distributing, and You must add the title, the copyright date, and the copyright holder's name to the COPYRIGHT NOTICE of any original Open Game Content you Distribute.

7. Use of Product Identity: You agree not to Use any Product Identity, including as an indication as to compatibility, except as expressly licensed in another, independent Agreement with the owner of each element of that Product Identity. You agree not to indicate compatibility or co-adaptability with any Trademark or Registered Trademark in conjunction with a work containing Open Game Content except as expressly licensed in another, independent Agreement with the owner of such Trademark or Registered Trademark. The use of any Product Identity in Open Game Content does not constitute a challenge to the ownership of that Product

END OF LICENSE

Made in the USA
Columbia, SC
30 November 2022

72423248R00052